HIDDEN
DRIVERS OF
SUCCESS

*Henry
long time coming! I hope you
enjoy!*

[signature]

Brian Morgan

Bill Schiemann

HIDDEN
DRIVERS OF
SUCCESS
Leveraging Employee Insights for Strategic Advantage

**William A. Schiemann,
Jerry H. Seibert, and Brian S. Morgan**

Society for Human Resource Management
Alexandria, Virginia
www.shrm.org

Strategic Human Resource Management India
Mumbai, India
www.shrmindia.org

Society for Human Resource Management
Haidian District Beijing, China
www.shrm.org/cn

The Society for Human Resource Management (SHRM) is the world's largest association devoted to human resource management. Representing more than 250,000 members in over 140 countries, the Society serves the needs of HR professionals and advances the interests of the HR profession. Founded in 1948, SHRM has more than 575 affiliated chapters within the United States and subsidiary offices in China and India. Visit SHRM Online at www.shrm.org.

Interior Design: Auburn Associates, Inc.
Cover Design: Auburn Associates, Inc.

Library of Congress Cataloging-in-Publication Data

Schiemann, William.
 The hidden drivers of success : unveiling the information power of your workforce / William A. Schiemann, Jerry Seibert, and Brian Morgan.
    p. cm.
 Includes bibliographical references and index.
 ISBN 978-1-58644-333-7
 1. Personnel management. 2. Communication in management. 3. Human capital—Management. 4. Knowledge management. I. Seibert, Jerry, 1962- II. Morgan, Brian S., 1942- III. Title.
 HF5549.S2236 2013
 658.3'14—dc23

                                                                    2012035925

ISBN: 978-1-586-44333-7   12-0626

Contents

Dedications

Bill Schiemann:
To a wonderful Metrus team for the past 25 years

Brian Morgan:
To Francine

Jerry Seibert:
To Jennifer, Jordan, and Nicholas

Preface

As the speed of global competition continues to accelerate, so does the need for precise, data-driven performance measurement. To allocate scarce resources, and to make course corrections and important business and talent decisions, fast and effective information is needed. We live in a world of data overload—for proof, go no further than your e-mail inbox! While data are over abundant, what is scare is having the right information available at the moment of decision-making truth. Even more scarce is the ability to convert data to knowledge for the purpose of organizational learning.

The idea for this book and its focus on surveys as a key tool to manage—even survive—in this competitive environment was incubated many years ago at the Metrus Institute. In our research, we have witnessed many superb examples of organizations that use information far more strategically than their competitors. So we began a quest to do three things that are integrated in this book:

- Examine great practices to understand how they came about—what leaders in those great measurement-practices organizations were doing differently; what were the unique aspects of their cultures that facilitated effectiveness; and what processes helped to produce superior information for decision-making.
- Conduct new and synthesize existing research to understand more about creating value. Why is some information

more powerful in key decisions? What are the leading and lagging indicators of performance and value? What is the relationship of talent and people in organizations to customer loyalty and retention, operational and financial performance? How can we use information to effectively anticipate and intervene in important outcomes, such as retaining top performers, improving quality or customer intimacy, or managing high potentials?

- Integrate what is out "there" in research and great practices into a framework for measurement that is helpful and applicable to both large and small organizations—for-profit and not-for-profit—and across industries and global environments.

The three authors began collaborating on this about five years ago, but their depth of experiences go much farther back, in some cases, to the 1980s. It has been interesting to see what long-standing measurement practices are still highly relevant and effective today, and to assess what practices have changed dramatically in the past three to five years. Our hope is to give you a state-of-the-art look at the practice of measurement—what is possible and what is likely in the future.

Acknowledgements

There are scores of people to whom we are indebted, including the many executives and managers who provided information and support along the way, from interviews—many in the past year—to research data and organizational practices. Also, while we remain responsible for the content of this book, there were so many people who influenced it in the design, review, and editing stages. In particular, we wish to thank the following people who provided a great deal of help: Thomas Belker of OBI Group Holding; Mark Blankenship of Jack in the Box Inc.; Steve Ginsburgh of Universal Weather & Aviation; Marisa Harris, author, speaker, and former Vice President of HR at CIT Group, Inc.; Robert Hoffman of Novartis Pharmaceuticals; Tine Huus of Nokia Corporation; Jim Leighton of Perdue Farms; Darren Smith, a senior executive in a federal agency; Melodee Steeber of Trustmark Insurance Company; Howard Winkler of Southern Company; Jeana Wirtenberg of Transitioning to Green; and the following Metrus Associates: Dave Allen, Susan Bershad, Laura Mindek, and Diane Schmalensee.

We also are greatly indebted to the Metrus Institute and Metrus Group for their generous support throughout this process, and to our colleagues who have been willing listeners and advisors as we came to grips with some of the tough measurement issues. In particular, we would like to thank two interns who provided invaluable research and literature review support: Shujaat Ahmed and Alex Garcia.

Also, Peter Tobia of Market Access and Christopher Anzalone, Book Publishing Manager at the Society for Human Resource Management (SHRM), were of invaluable help in supporting the idea of this book and providing the guidance, editing, and feedback that we needed along the way. We also want to thank the many folks at SHRM who collaborated with us to bring this book to fruition.

Colette Tarsan provided the essential coordination, prodding, and manuscript support, and we are greatly indebted to her for the high quality and timeliness of her work.

Finally, many thanks to our families for their great support during the difficult tasks of research, writing, and editing.

I

Unleashing the Power of Information

There is no doubt that information and knowledge separate world-class firms from the wannabes. The importance of and demands for real-time, evidence-based information has increased as the challenges of the new marketplace have accelerated: global competitors; technology advances; intensity of competition as suppliers exceed buyers; and the rising expectations of customers, employees, and shareholders.

Within the evolving business environment, a fundamental and growing challenge is the management and measurement of intangibles—such as company, product and employer brand, customer loyalty, employee engagement and alignment, ethics, innovation, effective partnerships, and culture.

Human capital is increasingly being viewed as the critical leverage point for managing these intangibles and as a major source of competitive advantage in the 21st century. Organizations that can harness, leverage, and optimize it will win in an increasingly fierce competitive environment. Organizations today are being squeezed by their competitors, customers, employees, and in many parts of the world by local and regional labor unions, regulatory agencies, and of course shareholders. After all, for most investors, the last decade has shown no increase in real income, riveting investors—whether private owners of medium and small businesses or large public corporation stockholders—on returns.

Rivals are making daily forays to attack your once unique competitive advantages. They compete for your best talent, top customers, and most effective suppliers. On the people side, for example, they set the bar on pay rates, perks, work/life balance, development opportunities, and many other factors. They hope to steal your best people, and why not? They are already trained and have demonstrated performance. You paid for recruiting them, screening them, developing them, and giving them experience. If you do not manage the human side of your enterprise, you will also be sending your talent on a farewell tour to your competitor.

Despite the recent recession, most developed countries are having difficulty finding skilled employees in fields such as nursing, trades, engineering, and the sciences. And whereas the recession has slowed Baby Boomers' retirements until they get their finances in order, it has also slowed opportunities in organizations for fast trackers and members of Generation X, who are looking to shape organizations in new ways. Also, fewer Millennials will be available to replace depleted skills, and many Millennials differ from their predecessors in terms of skill and career preferences; for example, they favor knowledge jobs over trades.

The Challenge

Winning in this new environment requires three critical ingredients:

- Strong and differentiated strategies
  - Clear focus on the "right" customer segments
  - Outstanding human capital or talent strategies
  - Strategies for managing other key stakeholders: suppliers, community, environmental, and so forth
- Great strategy execution
  - Strong alignment of stakeholders with organizational goals, values, and mission
  - The "right" core capabilities, including the right talent
  - Highly engaged workers
  - Adaptable and innovative people and systems to rapidly adjust to changing marketplace conditions

- Powerful measures to provide the vital, real-time information needed to make the scores of decisions required to navigate the turbulent environment and to implement the strategy successfully
  - Measures that provide outside-in information from customers and other external stakeholders
  - Measures that provide feedback on operating effectiveness and internal efficiency
  - Measures indicative of living important values, such as ethics, diversity, or health and safety
  - Measures of capabilities and how well they are being utilized—such as how well talent is being optimized
  - Measures of change, adaptability, and innovation
  - Measures that provide feedback on leader development and impact

Without effective, real-time strategic and tactical measures, decisions regarding strategy execution and a continuously shifting marketplace may be misguided or may lead to the waste of scarce resources. A few examples follow:

- Selection decisions based on ineffective interview and background information will result in new hires who fail or who create significant problems because they are misaligned with the organization.
- Optimized talent requires strong leadership capabilities. Without the right measures, managers without true leadership skills will suboptimize or even destroy talent in the organization.
- Waning supplier partnerships are likely to lead to poor input, less commitment to your success, and reduced value over time. Information is crucial to understanding how partners and suppliers are aligned with the organization's strategy.
- Failure to assess disengaged employees, teams, and departments leads to a vicious spiral, resulting in turnover,

dissatisfied customers, inferior quality, and poor operating results.

- High-performing employees with high-turnover risk profiles will be gone, assuming you do not have predictive indices *before* they leave.
- Internal service units without performance measures from their stakeholders operate inefficiently, resulting in higher financial burden and weaker organizational capabilities in the marketplace.

These are but a few of the many potential problems that result from poor information and knowledge management. The best firms have learned to harness the most beneficial information and to let go of much extraneous data that now overburden organizations.

This book will provide a framework for leaders to identify and extract crucial information to lead the enterprise, business unit, or department to success. Sadly, much of what is readily available is not necessarily the information needed for the best decisions, and the most useful information is too hard to detect, buried among thousands of data points. What may surprise you is that much of the information you need is often sitting nearby in the heads or on the desks of people around you, waiting to be tapped.

In this book, we will place particular emphasis on extracting valuable information from stakeholders in a timely fashion, thereby enabling leaders of all types to make great decisions. Many of your existing tools, such as surveys, were not designed or used to provide strategic decision information. We will show how various measures—with a particular emphasis on surveys—can be reinvented to serve today's strategic and operational needs. Although surveys have often been the domain of techies, today they are becoming the strategic intelligence network for top executives.

A principal area of focus is people. After all, people make most of the decisions in organizations—decisions about customers, products and services, supply chain, brand choices, ways to optimize talent investments, and productivity—while conserving scarce resources. And good decisions and effective resource allocation require the right information and knowledge. Howard Winkler, former Chair of the HR Certification Institute and Manager with Southern Company noted:

> Many business leaders are quite sophisticated in applying measures to the business functions they're most familiar with: financial measures, supply chain measures, or sales measures; but these same good leaders are often naïve when it comes to measuring other parts of their business, including human capital. Business leaders should demand the same disciplined and strategic thinking about measurement from the more intangible but equally critical parts of their business.

Thus, senior leaders will also need the support of a host of professionals who can help extract, design, understand, and use information in new ways. Because people are the centerpiece of organizational cost and opportunity, HR professionals will need to be ready to leverage these new tools. Other functional leaders such as CIOs, chief security officers, CFOs, or sales VPs have enormous opportunities to leverage the impact of their functions on the enterprise with the right people information, deployed in the right way. Statisticians, organizational psychologists, market researchers, and other specialty groups have an obligation not only to harness crucial data in their realm of traditional expertise but also to connect data points across the organization, using modern analytical tools, to enable senior leaders to manage the enterprise far more holistically than ever before. The days of having functional silos are over; today, we need horizontal information-rich enterprises.

The goal of this book is to expand thinking around how to use the richness of the information around us for the strategic benefit of the organization. In short, this is a book about managing organizational value—how to define it, how to measure it, and how to grow it!

Chapter 1

The Information Gap

"It was the best of times, it was the worst of times . . .
it was the spring of hope, it was the winter of despair . . ."
—Charles Dickens, *A Tale of Two Cities*

A Tale of Two Rentals

A few years ago, one of our authors (Schiemann) lost his wallet en route to a small Midwestern airport late one evening. As he headed from the terminal to the rental car agency, he had a queasy feeling, knowing he would have to explain his loss of identity to the service representative. But as a road warrior for many years, he had duplicate photo identification and another credit card tucked away in his suitcase, and besides, he was an "elite" renter.

He approached Cindi and Kim, the reps for the rental car agency, as they packed up for the night, knowing they had just one last reservation to deal with. Then came the dreaded question from Kim, "May I see your license please?" When our intrepid traveler pulled out his emergency backup, which incidentally had recently expired, she proffered the dreaded smirk and said, "You can't expect to rent a car here with an expired license."

After explaining the situation, the elite status, and the fact that he had rented about 25 times from the company that year, the deer-in-the-headlights look appeared as she slowly repeated, "Sir, you can't expect to rent a car here with an expired license."

At this stage, the road warrior moved on to Plan B, offering a few easy solutions. "How about looking me up in the computer?" After all, he had just rented one of their cars a few days ago. No dice. Apparently the computer system—or at least the operator—did not work that way.

Now our traveler was in Code Red—with no wallet and no cash, a taxi was not an option. On a last-ditch long shot, he asked to speak to the supervisor. The two quickly exchanged nervous glances, "No, we can't call her at home."

Our desperate traveler, on a tip from an airport manager, then tried a run at another rental car cube. Alex and Anthony gave him a different reception. After the traveler revealed his plight, these two superheroes went into action. They immediately logged in to their computer and identified his prior rental from many months earlier and then woke their manager at home to obtain special permission. Even when his emergency credit card came up "expired," they agreed to speak with the traveler's wife, by phone, who dictated another credit card number. By now, it was nearly 11:30 p.m. All the other cubicles were deserted, but Alex and Anthony had him driving out of the airport, despite all the setbacks.

What caused these two different experiences? Why did one team seem more interested in going home, whereas the other was inspired to extraordinary discretionary effort? If you were the CEO of the first company, how would you feel knowing your team risked the loss of a 30-year, loyal customer, especially when your competitor next door got the job done? Would you have wondered how many of your other employees are truly aligned with your values, brand, and strategy? Or were they indeed aligned with a culture that values no risk taking and has policies intended to avoid individual variation?

We experience these paradoxical service situations every day. And the impact of outcomes such as this are multiplied daily as customers tweet and post on Facebook. We start with this anecdote because it is fundamental to the story of success and failure in the new marketplace. It also raises the role of *measurement*, especially as it relates to human capital and other intangibles. Departing customers and their wallet share are measures that may indicate how good our strategy is and how well it has been implemented. Sadly, by the time these measures are noticed, analyzed, and reported, it is often late in the game. Reclaiming lost loyalties takes many years. Earlier indicators gathered through the eyes of employees or other sources are needed to identify gaps and to serve as early warning predictors of future customer or operational problems.

The rental car example is more than a story of great vs. poor service. It captures many of the key differentiators between successful and unsuccessful businesses today. Cindi and Kim may not have been highly *engaged*, or the *capabilities* simply were not there: training may have been inadequate, policies inflexible, and computer systems antiquated. Or possibly the company would have wanted them to bend the rules, but they did not understand or were not *aligned* with the values.

This book discusses a variety of ways in which measurement can be used more strategically and more decisively to gain competitive advantage—or for not-for-profits or government agencies, it is about reaching goals or achieving objectives more effectively and with less waste and frustration.

CEOs tell us they are urgently searching for answers to several core questions:

- Do we have a winning business strategy, and is it working?
- What do our customers think, want, or need?
- Are we effectively managing our risks?
- Do we have the right talent, and are we utilizing it well to execute the business strategy, to meet customer expectations, and to anticipate future customer needs or desires?

We have found that if we focus on these strategic questions first and deploy the right measurement systems to capture these core issues, other tactical decisions and measures will flow naturally from the answers. For example, focusing on these questions then leads us to important measurement decisions regarding internal functional alignment, supply chain management, labor relations, productivity, retention of top performers, talent acquisition enhancements, and a variety of other meaningful issues.

Is Your Strategy Working?

Strategies fail for usually one of two reasons: the wrong strategy or poor execution. How do we know if our strategy is a good one or that we are executing it well? *Strategy is about providing certain products or services to targeted customers based on a set of core capabilities in the context of a vision and mission.* The trick of course is identifying the right products or services, focusing appropriately on the right customers, and developing and utilizing these capabilities better than our competitors. The right measures will provide feedback on whether the strategy is a good one and how well we are executing it. Throughout this book, we will answer these essential questions, but to determine what we should be measuring, we first need to consider the strategic framework.

Framework for Making Strategic Decisions

Before discussing how you can become more effective in using measurement to reach your objectives, let us take a look at how measurement can play an integrative role in connecting strategy, customers, and the drivers of success for any business, regardless of size, region, or industry.

Figure 1.1 is a useful framework for thinking about how value is typically created in organizations and how the many stakeholders can make or break the success of an organization. Shareholder

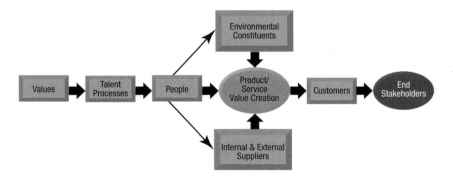

Figure 1.1 Framework for Value Creation

equity (or owner profit or "mission accomplished" for nonprofits or government agencies) is enhanced primarily by delivering products and services that have perceived value to customers or users in markets you have targeted. The ability to create those products and services is driven by effectively managing people, suppliers, and environmental constituents. We define the latter to include communities in which organizations operate, environmental stakeholders such as green or health and safety groups, and finally regulatory or other groups of influence such as unions.

This model allows for the varying strategic needs of different organizations. Rental car agencies, for example, must have their people—employees, contractors, managers—aligned with end stakeholders. Their suppliers range from tiny local repair operations to behemoths such as GM or Toyota that must support their strategy. And influential groups such as unions, airport authorities, or Consumers Union (the publisher of *Consumer Reports*) may influence their ability to deliver their products and services effectively.

If you work for a small organization, the same factors must be managed, albeit on a different scale. Your local auto repair shop owner, for example, has primary stakeholders, such as the owner's family, his customers, his employees, and the suppliers who get his parts delivered to meet customer promises. And periodically he must also deal with the township regulatory boards related to zoning issues or other community requirements. He must also comply with EPA and other federal regulations.

Consider some key stakeholders.

Customers

Customers can tell us a great deal about how the strategy works for them if we ask the right questions in the right way at the right time. They can tell us if they find our products valuable or competitive, provide ideas for what would enhance our value, or telegraph that our value proposition is fading. They can also tell us about execution. In the rental car example, if our co-author had been sent a follow-up questionnaire from the first agency after his experience at the regional airport, he could have reported on a range of areas, including computer glitches, employee attitude, employee competencies in observable areas, and adherence to hours of operation.

However, an often missed opportunity for firms is information from customers who walked away from a reservation and used a competitor. The renter did not show up in the customer transaction system that evening because he went to a competitor. Customers at a quick-serve restaurant who leave because of some problem before receiving the magic receipt that announces that they have been chosen for a service survey, or the potential customer who gives up during step 16 of a phone tree, are also among what we might call "invisible stakeholders."

Internal and External Suppliers

Internal functions. According to work that the Metrus Institute has done in conjunction with *Quality Progress*, the publication of the American Society for Quality, alignment and coordination of internal functions represent major gaps in many organizations. As any sales professional or customer service representative will tell you, his or her interaction with the customer will only be as successful as the suppliers that support them. Customers do not care about how the product or service reaches them—just that it does at the right time and at the right price.

Functional excellence and internal value delivery are two of the most under-measured areas. Some firms talk about a spirit of cooperation across all units—others about accountability for deliverables—but neither guarantees that high value is being created. Firms live or die in short order by whether the end customer sees high value, but they often miss the opportunity to deliver that value at lower cost.

Our research shows that firms and their functions vary widely in creating value, which we will discuss in more depth in Chapter 3. Those that excel at internal value creation have a competitive advantage in terms of employee retention, quality, customer loyalty, and financial performance. An organization's ability to deliver the value proposition to the customer and to fulfill the brand promise is only as strong as the weakest link in the value chain, including the many internal service functions that add or subtract value. By the time low value has been "felt" by the C-suite or other top managers, the function is often on the way to being outsourced.

Internal service metrics can be invaluable in helping to pinpoint the extent to which various functions within the organization are streamlined and synchronized. Are we producing great services, but perhaps at much higher costs than needed? Do functions cooperate with each other in effective ways to achieve end results, or is the organization riddled with silos that impede overall performance?

External suppliers. Measurement of supplier performance, either directly or through the eyes of employees, is often neglected. When a large pharmaceutical organization outsourced many of its clinical studies and large chunks of its clerical staff, it experienced a measurable shift in performance compared to when on-staff employees delivered those services. Many former on-staff employees became newly minted "supplier employees." They continued to work in the same location as before but received their paycheck from a different employer.

Now here is the interesting part. This pharmaceutical company suddenly stopped measuring the alignment, competency growth, and engagement of the employees who were no longer on payroll. The "burden" of the employees shifted to the supplier, and the process of measurement was shifted along with it. However, when clerical turnover started to increase, and employees no longer seemed to put in the extra effort, the pharmaceutical company was disappointed. Clearly, it had made these outsourcing decisions based on cost and perhaps risk mitigation, but the company lost its ability to predict and manage talent outcomes such as turnover or discretionary effort that was central to delivering quality results. The lesson here is that outsourced labor also need to be aligned, capable, and engaged.

Another missed opportunity is to ask employees about supplier issues. One pharmaceutical company we work with asked its employees questions about suppliers on its employee survey. For example, do employees think that the company allows suppliers an opportunity to make a fair profit? Obtaining the supplier's opinion would also be beneficial, but this is one more step to corroborate whether the firm's policies and actions support its values. We will address *internal function and supplier* issues, and their relationship to *customers*, in Section II.

Environmental Constituents

A variety of other stakeholders we call environmental constituents often play a role in organizational success. Among these may be the city council or mayor's office, safety regulators, green environmental groups, unions, consumers groups, and regulatory groups such as drug approval boards. Here, too, employees can tell us much about community relations, labor relations, regulatory risk, environmental challenges or successes, volunteerism, and much more. We will address some of the interesting challenges in managing and measuring areas such as sustainability and labor-management relations in Section VI.

People

People are the channel that connects operational systems, suppliers, and the broad environment stakeholders. We use the term "people" here rather than "employees" because most large organizations now use a variety of sources of labor in addition to employees alone: contractors, part-timers, consultants, outsourced or off-shored labor suppliers, and other variations. What is common across all these groups is talent. *The organization needs a pool of people who contribute a certain talent package that can be applied—with technology, materials, or processes—to provide products and services that customers want.*

Optimizing talent is the central challenge and key differentiator for most organizations. In this increasingly global marketplace, most organizations can access capital, materials, technology, or even world-class processes, but the people and their talent are what make two seemingly similar organizations perform differently. Talent determines whether the organization is innovative, efficient, productive, stable, ethical—ultimately, whether the organization will remain healthy and viable in today's and tomorrow's marketplace.

People also have a tremendous window on your customers. For example, sales and service employees have firsthand information about customers that can provide invaluable knowledge about market risks, customer expectations and levels of satisfaction, buying behaviors, areas of frustration, gaps in the product/service value offering, and numerous other issues.

Sales and service employees are not the only ones in an organization with a window on customers. Financial people often see other patterns, such as payment schedules (including risky late payers), credit worthiness, and the adequacy of financial information for customers. The IT department sees Web patterns. Manufacturing may understand back-order and delivery needs. And so forth. Put together, the data provide the organization with a fuller understanding of the customer, but each function within the organization must share and coordinate the information. In total, the data provide deeper insights; in fragments, they may send decisions down the wrong path.

Employees too can report on both the strategy and strategy execution. For example, the employees in our regional airport example have viewpoints about the company strategy, the alignment of their work with the group or company goals, the sufficiency of information or resources to do their job, the effectiveness of customer policies, and the clarity of communications.

The important part of employee feedback is that employees see what often lies below the surface and what is really going on. By asking the right questions and reviewing related measures, organizations may discern how well the strategy is being executed and what barriers lie in the way of improvement. Does the company have leading indicators that could have identified a risky situation *before* it happened? Was customer loyalty being assessed across locations, rather than in the aggregate? Was the rental car agency in our story identified as having low employee engagement or alignment by a strategic measurement tool? And if low morale was as an issue, did managers know the business drivers (not customers!) that caused it? Do they have a gauge of employee competencies relevant to customers? Though the answers are unclear, these are the types of informational issues that can make a huge difference to business success. We will explore many of these issues throughout the book. In Section III, we will address how strategic employee survey processes can provide far more strategic and decision-making information if they are designed, analyzed, and executed well.

Talent Processes and Values

Shown in the two boxes to the left of *People* in Figure 1.1 are *Talent Processes* and *Values*, both crucial to optimizing the performance of people and organizational success. Do employees believe their managers support the company direction, or are they just building their careers? Does the training work, and if not, why? Is the company selecting good talent who can serve the needs of customers? Are IT systems providing needed information for people to perform successfully? Are people willing to go the extra mile? Does the onboarding process tell them what they need to do to quickly become competent and successful in their jobs? In other words, do the *talent processes* work effectively—hiring the right people, acculturating them, optimizing their performance, developing great leaders, and retaining the best talent? We will explore these talent issues and how measurement can provide valuable insights in Section IV.

And finally, does the organization have the right set of *values*, and are they lived daily? In our rental car example, what are the values that the company wants to see exhibited, and what do employees see as reality? Do people buy in to the company values? Employees, and other stakeholders, provide a window into the organization's culture and reveal which values and behaviors are important day to day. Why were the employees of one rental car group willing to call their manager at a late hour whereas the other group was reluctant to do so? We will explore values such as ethics, diversity, inclusion, and innovation in Section V.

Once the groups that influence strategy and execution have been identified, the question is how each group will be monitored and measured so that it can be "managed" to the ends desired. For the small business owner, perhaps monitoring and measuring include tracking customer satisfaction, employee turnover and certifications, and zoning board changes. In the next chapter, we will discuss how we move from the more generic model in Figure 1.1 to a more specific strategy map that will point to the types of measures most valuable.

The Structure of the Book

The remainder of the book can be read sequentially, or you can jump to topics of special interest. In the next chapter, we address strategy and the role of measurement in capturing the major drivers of success. We will also challenge readers to compare what their organizations are doing today with a high-performance checklist.

In Section II, we look at performance through the eyes of internal customers as part of the overall supply chain serving our external customers. This section offers some of the greatest opportunities for even the most sophisticated information users today.

Section III recognizes the centrality of human capital in organizational success and the profound role of people in supplier and customer success. The section will begin with a look at the role of employees in the value chain and the role of people equity in capturing that value. The section will address a more traditional area that you may feel you know—the employee survey. However, we encourage you to browse this section carefully for new ideas because today's survey goes far beyond what management could have imagined in the days of traditional employee surveys. Today's survey is about using the eyes and ears of employees to optimize organizational performance and its use of talent. In this section, we will present several examples of companies that have reinvented the way they use employee information. The four chapters cover the following topics:

- Creating a *framework* or model for measuring your people
- Identifying *decision-rich data* needed in the context of your unique strategy and culture and gathering the data in ways that increase their validity and value; data today are ubiquitous, but there is a paucity of the right data and at the right time
- Extracting *information* from data that can be used for strategic business decisions, including analyses and interpretations that help prioritize resources
- Moving from information to *knowledge and impact*, overcoming a perennial problem that a vast majority of organizations face in driving new behaviors and making decisions

more effectively; knowledge and decisions are information that has been put to work

In Section IV we discuss using survey results and other information to manage the talent lifecycle. Most organizations invest the lion's share of their resources in managing the entire talent lifecycle. And yet, the measures often used to manage talent acquisition, onboarding, development, and retention are archaic and highly tactical. We introduce and explore the ACE framework in Section IV and use it to take a fresh look at how we can gain far better information and make more powerful decisions.

In the first chapter of Section IV, we take a look at *talent acquisition*—how can measures be more effectively used in managing your company and employer brand? How can we attract and select better talent who will be aligned with our organization, have the right competencies, and be highly engaged?

In the next chapter, we examine the other end of the talent life cycle—how can measures be more effectively used to *understand and predict turnover* and to strategically retain top performers? In the last chapter, we turn to leadership and performance optimization. How can measurement help us identify, develop, and retain stronger leaders—leaders who can optimize talent in their respective organizations?

Section V deals with a critical area for business today—values. Organizations are stumbling every day under ethical failures, diversity challenges, health issues, innovation flops, and other problems. Many winning organizations today utilize a values-driven approach to guiding decisions and behaviors—an approach that conserves resources and creates more effective decisions. We will look specifically at ethics, diversity and inclusion, safety, innovation, and other values that are crucial in most organizations.

Section VI looks into the Environmental Constituents box in Figure 1.1. In Chapter 15, we address the subject of labor relations and working with unions or other third-party groups that represent people. In Chapter 16 we discuss an issue gaining more relevance and visibility in organizational life: sustainability. This issue often involves many external constituencies such as environmental groups, government regulatory agencies, shareholders, nongovernmental organizations (NGOs), and formal and informal social groups. We will talk about economic, environmental, and social sustainability issues and ways in which employee measurement can provide valuable information in managing to sustainability.

Section VII peers into the future. How will we obtain information in a real-time, connected world? How can we better use employee and other information windows to make timely decisions? What would a strategic intelligence scorecard look like, and how might we obtain such information in cost-effective ways? In addition, we hope to challenge even the most sophisticated information users in our penultimate chapter on segmentation of the workforce. This chapter will introduce thinking from a variety of disciplines, discuss generational challenges and information, and provide recommendations on how you might mass-customize your workforce—the ultimate in matching people and organizational objectives!

Finally, Section VIII will close with a challenge, including an audit you can use in your own organization to test how well you are prepared for today's information challenges and where you might focus to better equip your organization for success. We will also aggregate the most salient *Action Tips* discussed throughout the entire book.

Chapter 2

How Much Do You *Really* Know About Your Organization?

"Our first priority was setting priorities."
— Jim Leighton, President, Perdue Foods

Organizations miss a good deal of the information they need to make necessary decisions. Where information does exist, it is often captured via many separate and fragmented methods, resulting in duplication, survey fatigue, waste, and disconnected information and limiting the ability to convert information to knowledge. The lack of a framework to codify the information in ways that can be shared to facilitate organizational learning is a major disadvantage.

In the second half of this chapter, we will provide a short assessment enabling you to assess how *information savvy* your organization is and how prepared you are to overcome the information challenges you face now and going forward.

Prioritizing the Priorities

One of the biggest challenges for any organization is focus. Identifying the priorities and managing them well are imperative. For most organizations, this means keeping a watchful eye on ten to twenty priorities. And for executives like Shivan Subramaniam, CEO of property insurer FM Global that employees 5,100 people, the priority list narrows to several core objectives or key results areas (KRAs):

profitability, client retention, and attraction of new clients.[1] All of FM Global's incentive plans are designed around the KRAs, which are very transparent. Subramaniam points out, "Most importantly, they [*all employees*] understand them, whether they're the most senior manager or a file clerk." Employees at every level know precisely how their actions influence each KRA.

As most firms do, FM Global focuses on two of the elements in Figure 1.1 found in Chapter 1—in this case, end stakeholders (the company's shareholders) and customers. In organizations, additional attention is needed to develop agreement among the leaders on what drives the KRAs. Although the model in Figure 1.1 provides a broad framework to prevent surprises, it does not help us stay focused on the "critical few" issues, and does not help ensure that we are not looking at far more customer and people attributes than we should measure. Our experience is that it is best to have some measures in place for every main stakeholder group, but not more than twenty measures in total. As one of our global energy clients said, "Twenty is plenty!" Most organizations, business units, or functions, will need fewer strategic measures that in turn can be supported by functional measures at the more tactical level.

In the early 1990s, Metrus pioneered the use of a concept called strategy or value maps that has been subsequently popularized as balanced scorecard maps and the like.[2] The purpose of these maps is to create a visual representation of one's overall strategy on a single page. The map included results on the right and drivers on the left, laid out in such a fashion that each concept (shown in Figure 2.1) is an outcome or driver of the other concept. For example, Growth in Net Income is driven by both Productivity and Growth in Revenue. A given concept may be an outcome of another upstream concept, and it may also be a driver of a downstream one.

The map in Figure 2.1, similar to Figure 1.1 in Chapter 1, identifies key elements of business performance—financial, customer, people, operations, environmental, supplier—that should typically be incorporated into a strategic measurement system. We will explore this map in more detail in subsequent chapters.

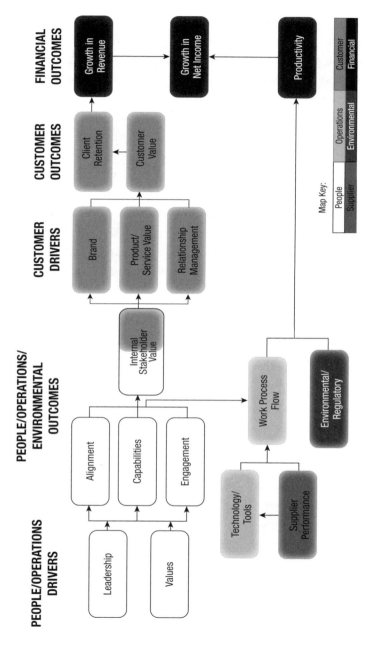

Figure 2.1 Strategy Map[3]

This map contains Financial, Customer, Internal Stakeholder, Operational, Environmental/Regulatory, People, and Supplier measures. If this map is built to represent the important value drivers of the business strategy, it will help focus attention on these factors. If each of these factors also has a sound measure, the organization will have a strategic intelligence system to balance the deployment of its resources to manage crucial stakeholders that can make or break the organization's success.

The map also represents a good balance between complexity and manageability. It contains enough factors to capture the real complexity of the business but not too many to overwhelm management. One of the major values of such a map is that tactical decisions (and measures) and organizational resources can be linked to these critical outcomes and drivers so that the organization optimizes its scarce resources.

Management Requires Good Measurement

As noted above, each of the factors in Figure 2.1 must be measured. Using one measure for each factor with clear targets for each is appropriate. These collectively become the scorecard at a strategic level and are often referred to as a dashboard at more functional or tactical levels.

Of course, tactical measures that support and are aligned with the more strategic ones will also be needed. These usually include organizational processes (for example, talent management, supply chain management, customer service), or capabilities (for example, R&D knowledge, innovation ideas) that support the scorecard areas and measures. For example, in the people areas, alignment will need to be supported by reward and performance management processes, knowledge of the business strategy, and company values. Engagement may be supported by supervisory training processes or policies that ensure fairness, diversity, and open communications.

In a variety of places throughout this book, we will discuss how to define the "right" measures and how you can use such information far more strategically and effectively than it has been used in the past.

Hard vs. Soft

Some of the items on the map are "hard" measures. For example, profitability, customer retention, and measures of work process and productivity fall into this category. Others are "soft" or intangible measures. Many of these can be captured reliably by surveys of stakeholders, including employees, internal customers, external customers, and suppliers. Because a large part of this book will be focused on intangibles that make or break your organization's success, surveys will be discussed as a focal tool. We will devote considerable space to the use of survey information because people's perceptions—whether external customers, internal customers, suppliers, or employees—make a crucial difference to the speed and accuracy of decisions. They tell us what has been done, is being done, and should be done and what is likely to happen in the future (for example, turnover, quality, customer spend, accidents). The better we can measure our stakeholders, the better we can manage our intangibles and our business success.

Surveys today have become mainstream tools for a variety of uses, but unfortunately, too often they are tactical, trivial, and overdone. In this book, we talk about some of the most powerful uses of surveys for strategic decision making in any business. You may be surprised by the potential uses of surveys that elude most organizations.

To provide an overview of the extent to which strategic surveys can be used to guide business decision making, consider the following checklist that indicates possible key measures for each of the items on the strategy map in Table 2.1.

An organization that has a strong strategic intelligence system will have measures from a variety of sources that provide the most effective feedback on issues essential to success. As noted in Chapter 1, we have found that employees in an organization have a phenomenal window on not only their own motivations and competencies but also on customers, processes, suppliers, and much more, as you will see as we move through the book. We will return to the value maps and scorecard issues in more depth in Section VII to address how one plans for, coordinates, and aligns a variety of measures to leverage the return on investment.

Table 2.1 Strategic Measurement Checklist

Strategic Measure	Measurement Tool			
	Employee Surveys	Stakeholder Surveys	Supplier Surveys	Other Measures
Leadership	●			
Values	●			
Alignment	●			
Capabilities	●			
Engagement	●			
Internal customer value		●		
Brand image		●		
Product/service value		●		
Relationship management		●		
Customer value		●		
Client retention				●
Supplier performance	●		●	
Technology/tools	●			●
Work process/flow	●			●
Environment/Regulation	●	●	●	●
Productivity				●
Growth in revenue				●
Growth in net income				●

Identifying Measurement Strengths and Gaps: How *Information Savvy* Is Your Organization?

A strategy map provides focus and enables the organization to identify measurement strengths and gaps. However, in our assessments of numerous organizations, we have found that gaps are widespread. At this point, let's explore some of the common gaps in critical areas to enable you to make a preliminary assessment of coverage in your organization.

In the process of preparing an employee survey for a global marketing firm, we asked for a data file with basic employee information, including e-mail addresses, to send out invitations. The chief human resource officer informed us that there was no employee database.

Each local office kept its own spreadsheet (he hoped), but the company had no central repository. He could not even tell us definitively what the total company headcount was without contacting a dozen office managers around the globe. Without a lifeline to communicate with employees from corporate, top management had to hope that everything was going according to plan. It was not. For example, when turnover problems soared, figuring out what was actually happening and why it was happening took months. When new hires left unexpectedly, the firm had no way to know whether the departures were related to overall company policies or to local management actions.

When you have to make a critical business decision, how often do you worry that your indicators may not be providing the best information about what is really going on? How often must you rely on tangential information? You must make the decision regardless, but the quality of your information can have a profound impact on your company's performance. Today, when organizations need every competitive edge, opportunity costs are often paid because we do not have the right information at the right time.

Consider the following issues, and ask yourself how good your current information is in each area. That is, do you have adequate information to understand each of these areas sufficiently to make optimal decisions?

- How well is your brand really doing? Would your workforce agree? Would your suppliers agree?
- How loyal are your customers? Would they stick with you if they were offered a "better deal?"
- Are you delivering the optimal value to the marketplace, given the resources you command?
- Are you getting optimal performance from your suppliers? Even if they are delivering what is expected, could they provide 120 percent of that under the right circumstances?
- Are your internal suppliers—your shared services or internal providers such as IT, Human Resources, Procurement, Security, R&D, upstream manufacturing, or service

groups—delivering optimal performance? Do you know if they could be more effective?

- Are your employees delivering maximum performance relative to their capabilities? Or are they just meeting annual goals? Are they developing the capabilities and competencies to meet tomorrow's goals and challenges or simply marking time?
- Do you have the innovation necessary to meet your goals? How would you know if you could obtain more for the same investment?

Each of these issues deals with broader organizational success. However, most of these issues are driven by your people—the talent in which you have invested to achieve the organization's goals. For most organizations, talent is the core of strategy design and execution. The talent in which you have invested innovates, executes, satisfies customers (or not) in a highly productive fashion (or not), and walks out the door every night. Fortunately, most of the talent comes back each day, but keeping the best talent is a challenge for any organization.

The following questions address this most important driver of success. Take a minute to answer the short assessment in Table 2.2 to see how well you are informed in areas related to your optimization of talent.

These statements should help you think about the types of decisions that must be made in most organizations and how effective your information sources are at getting you this information in cost-effective ways. Every one of these areas contains fundamental information for making better decisions that can help you edge out the competition and meet your desired vision, mission, and goals more quickly.

For example, the answer to the retention items will tell us how we can improve retention overall or the retention of top performers. Questions asked of employees who interface with customers will be good sources of information about changes in the customer base that are useful for product planning, forecasting, manufacturing,

Table 2.2 Talent Information Assessment

The following questions address the most important driver of success—the collective talent in which you have invested.

Answer each question below on a scale of Strongly Agree (5) to Strongly Disagree (1):

	Strongly Disagree	Disagree	Neutral	Agree	Strongly Agree
We have good information telling us how well we have optimized the talent we have invested in.	1	2	3	4	5
We clearly understand the root causes of why top performers leave the organization when they do.	1	2	3	4	5
We have good feedback systems from our own people to determine customers' loyalty and future needs.	1	2	3	4	5
We have information that provides a good understanding of how to best optimize performance of different cultural segments of our organization such as Gen Y's, minorities, or talent from different regions.	1	2	3	4	5
We have high confidence that we have identified the best high potential leaders in the organization.	1	2	3	4	5
We have good measures of our onboarding effectiveness.	1	2	3	4	5
We know how well our employer brand is doing in the marketplace.	1	2	3	4	5
We have good intelligence on why prospects turn down our job offers.	1	2	3	4	5
We have ongoing measures in place that tell us how well managers are optimizing the talent that they lead or coach.	1	2	3	4	5
We have information that tells us how to allocate our scarce leader development resources to optimize leader performance.	1	2	3	4	5

design, pricing, and service needs. Questions about talent turning down offers of employment will help your organization determine if the talent acquisition and employer branding processes are optimal and are providing the best talent and whether the branding message needs to change.

You might be surprised to find that all this information can be and has been obtained by best-practices organizations through surveys, which is why we put a premium on survey measurement in this book. Even more interesting is that over half the information could be obtained in one survey of employees because of their unparalleled window on customers, operations, suppliers, internal service providers, and their own position and attitudes. Whereas not all critical information can come from surveys of stakeholders, the reality is that strategic surveys can provide far more than most organizations realize.

In this chapter we have discussed how you can narrow your field of inquiry to those areas that are most strategic to your organization. Why ask about service if your organization does not value it as a competitive differentiator? Why add lots of questions on speed to market if you are in a mature market that is not competing on speed? We also learned the following:

- Many organizations are information poor regarding pivotal business and talent decisions. Each of those decisions may waste precious resources when not optimized.
- Whether your organization is large or small, you depend on many stakeholders for your success.
- Managing stakeholders, as well as other aspects of the business, requires good measures and timely feedback of information to make decisions.
- People are a core driver of most strategies but must work in concert with customers, suppliers, and other stakeholders to create value.
- Value maps help in understanding and communicating how value is created by the organization.

Next, we will turn to Section II, which will take a look at the customers and the supply chain.

Action Tips

1. Do you have a value map for your organization? If not, this would be an excellent start on the road to becoming measurement managed.

   a. Get together with colleagues to map out how value is created by your team or organization.

   b. Start by identifying the primary sources of value that you create (such as revenue, services, or risk mitigation) on the right portion of the map.

   c. For each value outcome, list the drivers that create that value on the left, as described in Figure 2.1.

   d. Ask: Does your model capture all the key stakeholders that can positively or negatively influence your strategy?

   e. Test your model to see if it is balanced. Does it include both short- and long-term value drivers? Does it include leading and lagging indicators?

   f. Test your model with other stakeholders to see if they see the same picture.

   g. Though having more than 20 drivers might be tempting— resist! Go back and ask yourself if you have captured the most important ones.

2. Do you have at least one sound measure for each driver and outcome on your map? If not, pull together a team to identify a good measure for each. For many of the areas, we will be addressing measurement ideas throughout the book.

II

FROM THE OUTSIDE IN

The leader of an internal service function once told us how the CEO's view of her function was driven by the perceptions of a few influential executives. More than once the CEO came down the hall into her office and challenged a recent action or program after hearing a negative remark from another VP. "If I didn't have data at hand to push back," she said, "those would have been very uncomfortable discussions."

Another frequent message we hear is, "I won't challenge your function if you don't challenge mine." Which really means that no measurement takes place and no one gets feedback until the situation is dire—when a critical mass of stakeholders is frustrated and angry. Good reputations are hard to build, but much harder to repair.

The question is, why does this type of situation happen? Delivering value is about more than doing good work and documenting it. A leader has the responsibility to ensure that the value of his or her function is clear to its stakeholders. That goal is not accomplished by sharing operational metrics in monthly meetings, nor is having an analysis at hand for responding to challenges sufficient. Leaders must systematically gauge and address internal customer needs and expectations.

Many functional leaders are not managing or measuring their function by the value it creates. How do you clearly and accurately understand customer requirements and expectations? How do you translate those expectations into value-producing products and services? How do you know that you are hitting the mark? In this section we will describe how suppliers—internal or external—can measure and improve value.

Chapter 3
Supplier Value Assessment

"Unless you get feedback on what you do, you will never improve."
—Steve Ginsburgh, Senior Vice President of Human Resources and Workforce Development, Universal Weather and Aviation

There is no room in modern corporations for an ineffective supply chain, whether it is internal or external to the organization. The competition is too intense and stakeholder expectations are too high to permit unchallenged expense or quality. Organizational boundaries are blurring as more companies have outsourced former internal departments such as Legal, Human Resources, IT, R&D, or Procurement, requiring external suppliers to become tightly integrated with the company, even housing members of supplier organizations within the company or building in tight communications links.

If internal functions cannot deliver operational excellence and a clear value to the organization, they are being outsourced, off-shored, or divided into more effective pieces. For example, some HR departments have found compliance shifted to Legal, Compensation moved under Finance, Recruiting outsourced, and so forth. The growth of outsourcing in particular has been extraordinary—in a survey of 2,000 companies, the Metrus Institute found that 94 percent had outsourced at least one of 15 major internal functions.[1] What began as an effort to shift low value activities to outside suppliers has steadily grown to the point where virtually any function may be subject to outsourcing: from Human Resources and IT to basic production and R&D. If internal products and services are to remain under internal departments, they must add higher value than can be obtained elsewhere.

Conversely, external suppliers may find that their work is being incorporated into the organization if the value of doing the work internally is perceived to be higher. At a Metrus Institute executive forum, Verizon, for example, described how it had brought back a number of externally supplied services, such as recruiting, into the organization in a number of countries in which the company operates.[2] In our study, one third of the companies reported insourcing a function that had been outsourced—a significant failure rate when you consider the time, effort, and cost of the outsourcing process. Whether external or internal, suppliers must provide high value to their end users. We will focus primarily on internal value in this chapter, but many of the points being made apply equally to both types of suppliers.

Internal customer service is a critical part of the service-value chain. The team in IT, for instance, may never see an outside client, but its inability to meet the needs of an internal customer in, say, a call center, has a direct impact on the ultimate customer. Similarly, if Human Resources fails in any of its core functions, the effects will ripple throughout the organization. Imagine the repercussions of a bad hire that Human Resources screened and approved or the negative long-term effects of a compensation system that does not reflect the organization's values, perhaps rewarding individual achievement at the expense of teamwork and cooperation. Our research has shown that companies with high levels of internal customer service deliver better internal value and are more than twice as likely to be leaders in their industry in terms of financial performance, productivity, and customer satisfaction, compared to companies with low levels of internal service.[3]

Defining and Measuring Value

Who knows better than you what will effectively deliver your department's main products or services? As the leader you have the deepest understanding of how your group functions and what re-sults it must achieve. Yet how you judge value and how your stake-holders judge it may not align. A common failing is to base an as-sessment of value and internal customer service on the metrics you have carefully designed to manage the operation. The mistake is in assuming those metrics also capture what is most important to stakeholders.

When reviewing the results of an internal value assessment with the worldwide leader of human resources in a *Fortune* 100 manufac-turer, we found that he was exasperated by the poor ratings of talent acquisition. The company had outsourced recruitment, and the sta-tistics related to a number of key performance indicators (KPIs) ran counter to the survey results. For example, the number of positions filled and time-to-fill KPIs were both tracking at the same or better levels than before the transition.

What the KPIs did not show was the frustration managers were feeling with the new supplier. The contract recruiters had none of the institutional knowledge the former in-house team had possessed, and they struggled to learn the markets for specialized engineers. Because they did not have a deep understanding of the company or the jobs, they pulled the managers into the hiring process much more often than the managers were used to. Moreover, high turn-over among the recruiters meant there was *always* a learning curve. Managers were aggravated, feeling they were doing most of the re-cruitment work themselves. However, this frustration never showed up in the traditional efficiency-focused recruitment metrics.

For any internal support function to support the value of the business, the needs and expectations of stakeholders must be clear. Internal value measurement enables the department to identify its service strengths and concerns, serves as a basis for setting improve-ment priorities in the areas that matter most to stakeholders, and provides a basis for ongoing performance tracking. For an internal value measurement initiative to succeed, it should be grounded in a clear vision of departmental objectives and use simple and user-friendly measurement tools.

4 Steps to Improve Internal Value

In the end, the assessment is not what matters as much as what you do with the stakeholder feedback. But good information is the foundation for action. How do your stakeholders assess the value of your department's products and services? A comprehensive method for internal value assessment has four steps.

Step 1. Planning and Defining

To begin, consider the department's mission and objectives. What are your service goals? Have you set service standards? What are the core services you provide—the deliverables that add value? You also need clear definitions of chief stakeholders, understanding that their needs may differ. Here we borrow an idea from market research: market segmentation. Any internal service provider has a number of distinct segments:

- *Funders*: These are the real decision makers regarding your budget and approved initiatives.
- *Influencers*: These may be peers, other leaders, or managers whose opinions are trusted and respected by others.
- *End users*: These make direct use of your services; they may be at many levels of the organization and for groups like IT and Human Resources include the general employee population.

The needs and expectations of these "market segments" are going to be very different, but function leaders rarely invest the time and effort to clarify those differences *and* apply that knowledge to reengineer their deliverables and communication strategies.

For example, consider a new training program for customer service representatives—its value is different for each market segment. You need to show *funders* the initiative moves the organization closer to strategic goals: Improved complaint resolution means higher customer loyalty, which converts directly to bottom-line impact. For the influential head of customer service, the new training program may mean fewer escalations to supervisors, who will then have more time for coaching, helping the call center meet its goals. For *end users* (the trainees in this case), the value may be lower stress from being better able to defuse issues with dissatisfied customers. The metrics and the message to convey value will be different for each group, which in turn will influence the focus and methodology of your assessment.

Now is also the time to candidly discuss known and suspected customer service issues. Addressing these directly in your assessment sends a message that you are serious about internal service.

Who should be included in your assessment? At a minimum, all the *funders* and a sample of *influencers*. The focus of your assessment will determine whether *end users* should be included. Many internal value assessments focus on managers and executives, whereas assessments for *end users* are often tailored to a specific service encounter (such as a security incident or a training program). You need to consider if the evaluations you request can really be provided by all *end users*, or whether a more targeted approach is appropriate, with *end user* input coming through other mechanisms to round out your feedback.

Step 2. Assessment

Candid conversations with key stakeholders are important. If approached in a structured and open-minded manner, striking insights can be gleaned, and a better understanding of the stakeholders' definition of value can be developed. The problem is that for many leaders conversations constitute the whole of their customer outreach. We asked managers at over 1,200 organizations what methods (if any) they used to assess internal value. Almost all said they met regularly with leading stakeholders. Only about half used a more formal, structured method such as surveys or incident-tracking databases.[4]

Unfortunately, those periodic conversations are not enough. We examined the internal service levels across those 1,200 companies. Then we compared departments that relied on just talking with stakeholders with those that also used one or more of the systematic approaches. *Those taking a rigorous, measurement-based approach had significantly more favorable internal service ratings.*

There is certainly value in talking to *funders* and other key leaders, but theirs is just one perspective. As useful as their comments may be, keep in mind that *the plural of anecdote is not "data"*—that is, a few stories or examples may not be fully representative of all of your market segments. Eliciting feedback from a wide range of managers and employees, a cross-section of *all* your stakeholders, is the only way to achieve a full, 360-degree view of your function's internal value. A well-designed internal value assessment (IVA) can quickly deliver a wealth of insights without burdening your stakeholders or significantly diverting your own resources (or budget).

To maximize insights, you need to conduct a survey that includes questions that allow stakeholders to evaluate the major services you provide—your core deliverables. Sometimes gauging the familiarity of those deliverables is also useful; if people do not fully understand or are not aware of your primary functions, you have some educating to do internally. Let your stakeholders know in advance what you will be doing and why. Promote the survey at department head meetings; mention it in your company newsletter. The higher the profile, the more responses you will get back and the better the data you will have to work with.

We all want a pleasant experience when we interact with a supplier—internal or external. A likeable staff that tries hard can make up for many failings . . . at least for a time. But do not make the mistake of assuming friendly service equals stakeholder satisfaction. At a northeastern utility, we found one of the most pronounced examples of "good service but low value" feedback we have ever seen. The function we worked with had fantastic ratings on a wide range of service dimensions. Service representatives in the function were always available, courteous, and personable, and they returned calls. They were indeed a nice group to work with. Their stakeholders did not hesitate to praise them for these characteristics. On some measures they topped out our database: 15, 20, even 25 percentage points above our comparative performance norm.

On the other hand, many of the service representatives had moved into the department from other parts of the company and were chosen for their interpersonal skills. Few had any professional training or certification in the field. Over time, the lack of base skills and knowledge compounded. Errors were common. Projects were behind schedule. Most of their core deliverables were actually rated below the norm. One manager described the staff as "respectful and professional, even when they cannot deliver." Worst of all, the higher we went in the organization, the greater the level of dissatisfaction expressed ("nice" typically does not cut it with executive teams).

How you interact with your internal customers will greatly influence their assessments. Discovering issues with availability, timeliness, professionalism, and the like is helpful, yet in the end it is *what* you do that matters most. You have to deliver on your major responsibilities.

A well-designed assessment will therefore include a focus on both what you do (the core deliverables) and how you do it (dimensions of service interactions). Table 3.1 lists a few examples of core deliverables for some common departments, as well as service dimensions that may apply to any department.

Step 3. Analysis and Priority Setting

With the above framework and information in hand, you can identify service performance levels, strengths, and gaps. Work with your

Table 3.1 Examples of Core Deliverables and Service Dimensions

Core Deliverables: "*what you do*"		Service Dimensions: "*how you do it*"	
Human Resources	Talent acquisition	Trust	Available when needed
	Compensation and benefits management		Reliable—follows through
Finance	Budget reports	Competencies	Accurate
	Forecasts		Knowledgeable
Security	Incident response	Business acumen	Understands business needs
	Event security		Proactive
IT	Help desk	People equity (ACE)	Alignment with organization priorities
	Intranet management		Capabilities—has the required resources
			Engaged—willing to put in extra effort

team to select priorities for action. With stakeholder feedback documented in black and white, most teams will quickly move past denials and excuses and on to the critical stage of identifying and prioritizing opportunities.

Internal value assessments do not require a great deal of advanced statistical analysis. The focus should be on easily understood data displays such as averages, percentages, and bar charts. Such displays are effortlessly explained and understood by the entire team. Figure 3.1 shows an example of a typical display for a question from an internal value assessment. With this type of reporting, one can see differences between stakeholder groups and whether they represent different management levels, regions, or business units.

What are the most visible gaps? First consider the results in the context of your strategic priorities: Do goals for your function take precedence because they are integral to the company's strategic goals? Next, which issues are most consequential to your stakeholders? This value may be assessed by incorporating "importance" ratings within the survey or through a statistical driver analysis. The latter approach tends to be more effective because space limitations preclude the inclusion of low-importance/low-value deliverables in most assessments. As a result, self-report importance ratings tend to indicate that everything is "important." A driver analysis, on the other hand, may tell you conclusively that certain core deliverables or service dimensions have a much greater impact on judgments of value.

An example of one type of priority matrix is shown in Figure 3.2. In this example performance is represented as a comparison against an external benchmark (vertical axis) with importance (derived from a driver analysis) on the horizontal axis. In addition, the relative degree of "familiarity" to the stakeholders is indicated by the size of each bubble. This analysis reveals that talent acquisition and retention, as well as timely service, are leading opportunities for this HR department, whereas succession planning and training and development are real strengths.

Having comparative data available can be helpful. We have observed a wide range of ratings for different types of core deliverables

Question	Group	N Size	Percentage of People Responding		Percentage				
				VG	G	Avg	P	VP
14. Human Resources **responds** to your requests in a **timely** manner.	Overall	2477	70% 22% 8%	28	42	22	6	2
	Business Unit							
	Consumer	1111	60% 40%	20	40	40	0	0
	Automation	724	89% 11%	11	78	11	0	0
	Materials	209	56% 28% 17%	33	22	28	11	6
	Research	251	43% 57%	7	36	57	0	0
	Corporate	182	73% 18% 9%	27	45	18	9	0
	Key Stakeholders:							
	Senior Leadership	21	71% 17% 12%	42	29	17	4	8
	Division leadership	142	71% 29%	7	64	29	0	0
	Managers	2312	62% 26% 12%	22	40	26	10	1
	Region							
	Asia-Pacific	459	50% 33% 17%	28	22	33	11	6
	Canada	67	64% 36%	14	50	36	0	0
	EMEA	486	88% 12%	25	63	13	0	0
	Latin America	91	33% 17% 50%	0	33	17	50	0
	US	1374	69% 25% 6%	19	50	25	6	0
	Metrus Norm		45% 37% 18%					

Figure 3.1 Variance Among Stakeholders

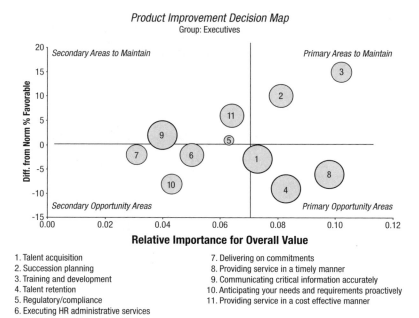

Figure 3.2 Product Improvement Decision Map

and service dimensions. For example, being proactive and anticipating stakeholder needs are much more challenging than being knowledgeable or providing timely service. Having the context of ratings from similar functions in similar organizations helps put results in perspective.

What causes each gap? Root cause analysis can help you determine the underlying causes for service problems. There is almost always a quick and obvious cause to be identified, and it is usually not correct. Applying the "five whys" can be effective: Once a surface cause has been identified, explore whether additional causes may exist. Then for each first level cause ask why it happened. After three to five levels of "why," you will find that you are much more likely to have arrived at the true root cause.

What solutions can be used to address each cause? What targets should be set for improvement? Brainstorming by the team is the best way to develop initial solutions. The most preferred source of process and service improvement is almost always from the people most closely involved in delivering the services. However, given that the ultimate goal is to increase the value for your key stakeholders, any potential change or action should be previewed with at least a few of those stakeholders. Sometimes a change will have unforeseen implications for a stakeholder, so identifying in advance any potential speed bumps will make implementation much smoother.

Sometimes the expectations of stakeholders are not aligned with the role of the department or with the reality of what is possible. In such cases, the outcome will be education focused. Clarifying what the deliverables are (and are not) or communicating constraints can go a long way toward resetting expectation levels. For example, an HR department was struggling with low ratings on timeliness for recruitment. Senior management had intentionally imposed an extra (and time-consuming) level of approval for all positions in developed markets because it wanted workforce growth to be targeted toward developing markets. But globally, that fact had never been communicated to managers. Because accelerating hiring decisions in the developed countries was not possible, human resources began a communication process that would give managers in those countries a more realistic estimate of the time to get positions approved, the probability of approval, and the strategic reason behind the situation. Gradually, ratings improved as awareness of the new reality took hold.

One solution that teams rarely raise is improving their own level of alignment, capabilities, and engagement; perhaps focusing on process improvement is less threatening. However, in our study of 2,000 companies, we found that when employee engagement was low, there was poor internal service, indicated by 20 percent to 40 percent favorable ratings for overall service quality. Internal service was significantly higher when employees were highly engaged, averaging 35 percent to 60 percent favorable. But the most impressive levels of internal service were demonstrated by those organizations that not only had high engagement but that also demonstrated high levels of workforce alignment and capabilities. Those organizations averaged a spectacular 70 percent to 90 percent favorable. Figure 3.3 illustrates these results. We will talk more about the combined power of alignment, capabilities, and engagement in the next chapter.

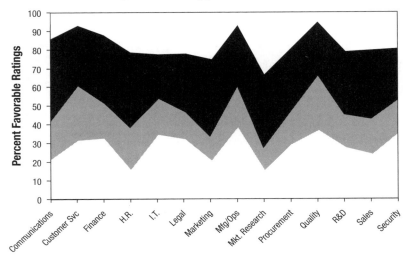

Figure 3.3 Internal Service Ratings and Engagement

Step 4. Focused Improvement

Now comes the payoff: implementing improvement plans that have been driven directly by your stakeholders. Just going through the process will likely change how you are perceived by senior management. Now imagine being known as the group that *proactively* anticipates the requirements of other departments and really *understands* their business needs.

To accomplish real improvement, you will need to develop and implement formal action plans. One of the keys to successful action plans is to keep them highly targeted. Even if your assessment identifies a wide array of improvement opportunities, selecting no more than two or three for action is best. Launching too many initiatives invariably leads to slower progress and, worst case, abandoned efforts. By focusing on just a few opportunities, you can achieve some great results for the team and demonstrate your commitment to internal value for all your stakeholders.

External Suppliers

Much of this methodology can be applied to external suppliers. Although an external supplier may be more likely to have some structured stakeholder assessment of its own in place, such assessments are usually limited to issues specific to a formal service level agreement (SLA). They often fail to comprehensively address the issues meaningful to the full range of stakeholders in the client organization. SLAs are tightly defined contract documents focused on specific aspects of work processes, aspects that the supplier can be held accountable for, and to some extent compensated on (or penalized on). Thus, to gain the most valuable information for you and the supplier to achieve the best value in the relationship, a complete assessment of core deliverables and service dimensions is recommended.

Conclusion

As Darren Smith, a measurement specialist for a federal agency, explained:

> The perceptions of *funders* based on informal feedback they receive on the quality of internal service delivery will make or break an internal supplier. The simple question for an internal service provider to ask *funders* is, "What do you need from me so that you can meet your operational objectives?" This sets the foundation for the conversation which is customer focused and implicitly delivers value. Rigorous measurement is helpful on two fronts: It demonstrates to production organizations that the internal corporate function is exercising due diligence in running itself like a business and it allows for process improvement to deliver higher value.

A periodic value assessment will benefit your department, your company, and probably your career. You will better meet the needs of employees, managers, and executives. Receiving the feedback may not always be pleasant, but you can be sure that when you listen and respond to stakeholders, your value only goes up.

Action Tips

1. Do not rely solely on anecdotal feedback from your internal customers. Implement a systematic approach to identify key stakeholder groups, clarify their expectations, and measure their level of satisfaction with your department's deliverables.

2. When gaps are found between expectations and satisfaction, first determine if expectations are realistic. If not, educate your stakeholders. If gaps exist, improvements in competencies, processes, or resources will be needed.

3. Always go back to your stakeholders after an internal value assessment to let them know what you heard (both the good and the bad) and what your plan of action is. It is a way of demonstrating that you are following through on the implicit promise made when you asked for their input.

4. If you are an external supplier, negotiate access to a broad range of stakeholders in your client organization. Then conduct a complete value assessment proactively. Your interest in delivering the greatest value for multiple stakeholder groups will send a powerful message to your clients.

III

FROM THE INSIDE OUT— USING PEOPLE EQUITY AND STRATEGIC INFORMATION TO MAKE BETTER DECISIONS

A well-designed and conducted employee survey is the centerpiece of an organization's strategic people measurement system. As indicated in Chapter 2, talent management issues and the people measures that support them are leading indicators of the organization's performance in many critical areas, including customer, operational, and financial performance.

In this section we explore the People Equity model, a framework for understanding talent issues and optimizing talent investments. The model is built on three key dimensions: Alignment, Capabilities, and Engagement (ACE). Taken together, these dimensions provide a foundation for building a strategic people measurement and management system closely linked to business performance. People Equity is covered in Chapter 4.

Once People Equity has been introduced, we turn to the strategic employee survey, a tool for people measurement that provides management with information to guide decision making on major talent issues. Because of the criticality of the strategic employee survey, we devote three chapters to it.

Chapter 5 on survey planning and design examines steps that need to be taken at the beginning of the survey process to ensure that the questionnaire covers the appropriate issues and, most significantly, that senior management is on board with the survey and is prepared to use it as a tool for decision making. This approbation requires a process for involving senior management in survey design, which we also explore in Chapter 5. By grounding the survey in company strategy and working with senior management to define the people issues necessary for achieving strategic objectives, surveys become transformed into a strategic tool for key decisions. By integrating an organization's strategy with People Equity thinking, the content of strategy questionnaires and related processes becomes redefined. This chapter also provides guidance for the issues that surface as a result.

Chapter 6 on turning data into insights examines how the analysis of the survey findings can transform employees' responses into strategic business information. Packaging is one of the pertinent considerations: How should we display survey information in ways that are easy to understand and that command managers' attention? State-of-the-art analytic tools for identifying drivers of overall Alignment, Capabilities, and Engagement levels are explored, as are tools for linking employee survey findings to business outcomes such as turnover, customer satisfaction and value, and financial performance. Segmentation of survey findings to provide profiles of key groups of employees, including high-potential employees and high performers, is also examined. Segmentation is considered again in depth in Chapter 19. Finally, a guide is provided for managers for priority setting that enables them to home in on the most critical people issues for action in response to the survey.

Chapter 7 deals with turning insights into business results. It explores the requirements for successful implementation of follow-up action on surveys. The chapter focuses on five elements critical to success. One or more of these are almost always missing in organizations, greatly reducing the impact of the survey information. This chapter will discuss how we can overcome these challenges.

Chapter 4

Optimizing Talent

"The ACE framework helped us understand how we were executing our strategy and how we could optimize our talent investments."

—Mark Blankenship, Senior Vice President and Chief Administrative Officer, Jack in the Box Inc.

Tom Hopkins is a top-performing restaurant manager with a major quick-serve organization. Revenues for the restaurant are over $110,000 per month; profits are solid; crew turnover is 20 percent lower than the average for other stores; and the company receives fewer than five complaints for every 1,000 customer transactions. Quite a performance! In contrast, Helen Hu, Tom's peer who manages a restaurant in the same region, is struggling. Monthly revenue barely tops $80,000; her company receives more than 25 complaints per 1,000 transactions; and crew turnover is well above average. She is among another group of restaurant managers who fit similar profiles. If you were a senior executive for this firm, what hypotheses would you put forward to explain the difference in performance?

Most leaders we know are apt to point to several factors to explain the difference, such as the following:

- Training of the managers
- Inheriting good or poor performers
- Inheriting a good or poor local market
- Hours worked
- Bad and good luck

In this company and many others, the above factors serve more as excuses for the problems than for addressing the real issue: how employees are managed to achieve peak performance. In this organization, all managers are trained alike, and employees are hired, trained, and paid using the same corporate policies and processes. Restaurant managers work the same number of hours, and customer demographics are identical. And the better the managers are at optimizing their people, the more effective they are.

This is one of many examples of how one organization excels another by the way talent is led and optimized.

What Do We Mean by Optimizing Talent?

Research by Schiemann and his colleagues[1] has shown that three factors account for much of what it takes to achieve peak performance:

- *Alignment*—Are all employees rowing in the same direction and synchronized across different interdependent teams?
- *Capabilities*—Do employees have the skills, information, and resources to meet customer expectations?
- *Engagement*—Are employees not only satisfied, but are they committed, energetic advocates for their organization?

These three factors—we refer to them collectively as ACE or People Equity—have been shown to be key for producing results: higher productivity, lower turnover, higher customer satisfaction and loyalty, improved quality, better internal customer service, and stronger operating and financial performance.[2]

An example of these results is summarized in Figure 4.1.

In the physical world, there are two forms of energy: potential and kinetic. *Potential energy*—like that in a battery—is stored so that it can be unleashed to serve a specific purpose, like starting a car. *Kinetic energy* is the energy of motion. A bow in the drawn position has potential energy; when released, the arrow has kinetic energy (motion), which creates an impact—perhaps a hole in the bull's-eye of a target!

You can think about people and their collective talent in a similar vein. People can have *potential* residing in their job, career

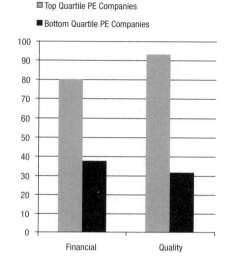

Companies with high ACE

✓ Were **2x** more likely to be financial leaders in their industry

✓ Were **3x** more likely to be quality leaders in their industry

✓ Averaged half the turnover of low ACE companies

Figure 4.1 Example of People Equity Results
Sources: J. T. Kostman and William A. Schiemann, "People Equity: The Hidden Driver of Quality," *Quality Progress,* May 2005, 37-42.Jerry H. Seibert and John Lingle, "Internal Customer Service: Has it Improved," *Quality Progress,* 2007, 35-40.

experiences and education, their relationships with others, their capacity for work, or their commitment to an organization. They may have potential for additional projects, skills, or new behaviors, but it must be converted to productive use—kinetic energy—to be valuable to the organization. Think of People Equity as a reservoir of people capacity, some of which is being used now and some of which is in the ready for future use. Effective organizations tap into this kinetic energy all the time to accomplish goals; smart ones also continue to build the right potential energy for the future.

People Equity is about finding the right mix—that is, optimizing talent so that it is neither wasted nor sitting on the shelf draining its value—like a battery over time.

The higher the People Equity, the more productive energy you have to achieve your goals and to build a reservoir of future potential. Just like other assets, such as financial or customer loyalty, People Equity can be depleted over time because the organization drains more from the reservoir than it replaces. Organizations that fail to pay as much attention to People Equity assets as they do to financial or capital assets will slowly diminish their capacity to perform and compete in the marketplace.

The quick-serve restaurant chain cited at the beginning of the chapter targeted 100 restaurants that were in the red—those having low People Equity—and in so doing was able to dramatically improve the performance of those operations. Metrus Group uses "green" for high people equity, "yellow" for medium, and "red" for low. For an average restaurant that goes from red to green—low to high People Equity—the improvement is worth about $200,000 in revenue, $100,000 in additional profit annually, and $60,000 in direct retention and churn costs. As you can see, there is a strong incentive to create high People Equity organizations.

Can People Equity Be Managed?

To manage People Equity—or ACE—organizations must be able to control the things that influence People Equity. Figure 4.2 shows the five drivers and four enablers of People Equity (see descriptions of

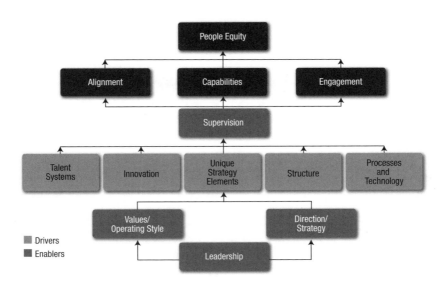

Figure 4.2 People Equity Drivers and Enablers

these in the sidebar below). The five drivers are identified as such because they typically have a more direct effect on one aspect of ACE. For example, two of the Talent Systems, performance management and rewards, have the most direct impact on Alignment. Technology, in contrast, has the most direct impact on Capabilities.

In contrast, the four enablers tend to influence all aspects of ACE. The supervisor or immediate manager, for example, is the day to day influencer of ACE. He or she influences Alignment, for example, by how goals are set, performance feedback is given, and rewards are doled out. Capability is influenced by enabling necessary information, building good teamwork, and increasing the skills of individuals, for example. Engagement is enhanced by good communication, fair treatment with respect, and recognition among other drivers.

Top leaders also influence all three areas of ACE because of their personal behaviors as role models, how they communicate the company strategy and values, and their control or influence on the performance of many of the drivers. For example, pay policies are often set by top management. The organizational structure is created by this group, and it strongly affects technology investments and innovation.

Combined with the value of the actual business strategy in setting a winning direction and the corporate values, the immediate manager and top leadership have a major influence in creating high or low ACE organizations.

Measuring ACE

Managing what you cannot measure is difficult. The good news is that ACE is quite measureable. After extensive research by the Metrus Institute and other researchers, the authors discovered that the desired ACE characteristics could be directly or indirectly measured through a specially designed employee survey. Organizations can corroborate additional aspects of ACE through interviews, focus groups, archival reviews, alignment audits, and such. However, the core ACE survey has the advantage of providing a standardized instrument with norms that allow comparisons across A, C, and E on a common 100-point scale. This approach gives an organization the

Examples of Content in People Equity Factors, Drivers, and Enablers	
Factors of People Equity	
Alignment	• Clarity of strategy; understanding of and alignment with goals • Alignment of values • Synchronization of processes and functions to deliver value to customers
Capabilities	• Skills and knowledge to meet customer requirements • Resources to meet customer requirements • Sufficient information to meet customer requirements
Engagement	• Employee commitment and satisfaction • Willingness to advocate on behalf of the organization • Willingness to give extra effort
Drivers of People Equity	
Talent Systems	• Recognition and rewards • Talent acquisition and development • Performance management
Technology Systems	• Operations and process drivers • Process effectiveness • Adequacy of performance tools • Effectiveness of knowledge management and information use
Innovation	• Idea production and use • Creativity • Adaptability
Structure	• Staffing adequacy • Cross-functional information flow • Functional silos
Unique Strategy Elements	• Customized to the organization's strategic priorities
Enablers of People Equity	
Direct Supervisor or Manager	• People skills • Technical skills • Performance management skills • Communication
Leadership	• Direction setting • Confidence in leadership capability • Walking the talk
Direction/Strategy	• Clarity of strategy • Strategic measures
Values	• Core values • Custom values

ability to compare itself to perfection, to best-practices organizations, or to itself over time.

Additionally, an ACE survey can be customized to include distinct aspects of the organization, enabling survey feedback to be even more specific to the unique strategy, values, and goals of the organization. For example, take the restaurant group that we have been discussing. Rather than simply asking how well employees understood the business strategy and its connection to them, the group tested that understanding on three specific aspects of the business strategy. Likewise, rather than talking about values in general, we can measure how well people in the organization believe in or see others adhering to specific values, such as ethics or diversity.

Much more on the measurement of these concepts will be addressed in subsequent chapters in this section.

A Picture is Worth a Thousand Words

Figure 4.3 displays a satellite view of how a global consulting firm has optimized its human capital.[3] The higher the scores, the more successful the organization has been at leveraging talent investments at all levels.

The beauty of this display is that it allows leaders to quickly assess their talent landscape and risks. For example, in this exhibit, the US Northeast is an area with perhaps some best practices that can be adapted to other groups. This area is leveraging its human capital investments well. In contrast, EMEA is a region that is challenged on multiple fronts.[4]

A particular profile may have more than one root cause. In a recent survey for an electric utility, low Engagement scores in the security organization were strongly driven by low recognition and fear of speaking up, whereas in its IT organization low Engagement scores were strongly driven by workload. By understanding these profiles, leaders and managers can take actions to improve performance in each discrete unit, thereby increasing overall People Equity—and customer and financial performance.

The Eight Talent Profiles

Table 4.1 displays eight profiles that capture the various combinations of high and low A, C, and E scores, each requiring different

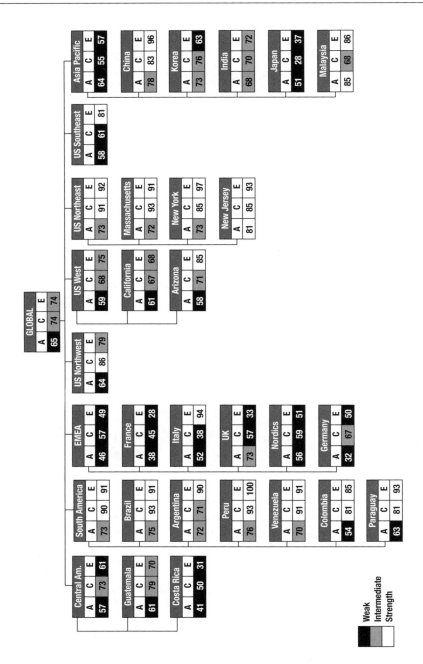

Figure 4.3

Table 4.1 People Equity Profiles

Alignment	Capabilities	Engagement	Profile	
⬆	⬆	⬆	Optimized Talent	
⬇	⬇	⬆	Misguided Enthusiasm	Suboptimization
⬇	⬆	⬆	Strategic Disconnect	
⬆	⬇	⬆	Under Equipped	
⬆	⬆	⬇	Disengaged	
⬆	⬇	⬇	Unable/Unwilling	
⬇	⬆	⬇	Wasted Talent	
⬇	⬇	⬇	High Risk	

⬆ High   ⬇ Low

actions and possibly leader development. For example, you have probably experienced the Under Equipped profile when visiting a retail store or booking something with an online sales representative. If you worked with a rep who seemed aligned with the values of the organization and high-energy but did not seem to understand your issue or was having problems getting his or her computer to fulfill your order correctly, you were most likely experiencing this profile. A leader of a unit with this profile might be blind to needed resources or to knowledge required to meet customer expectations. Such a situation may signal investments in training, orientation, coaching, or perhaps better technology.

In contrast, the Strategic Disconnect is a dangerous profile because people look like they are working hard, but odds are they are not working as smart as they could be. They may be diverting precious time and energy to side issues or to lower priorities or attending to distractions. This scenario often leads to wasteful overstaffing, frustration of the staff at not having enough resources (because they are not as focused on the priority tasks or willing to give up the lower-priority tasks), missed goals, or burnout as they are running faster on a runaway treadmill. One government energy group faced this challenge. As the funding dried up in some areas and project teams were directed to divert their energies to other projects, some units did not give up doing what they really liked on the projects that lost funding, resulting in weak results in the new priority areas.

Or take the Disengaged profile, a frequent one in more mature businesses. Units with this profile have employees who are often talented and know what should be done but are cynical and feel that the organization has not done right by them. Perhaps this profile results from years of being ignored, as we saw in an engineering organization with professionals who became jaded due to poor technical investment decisions, a lack of listening, and inadequate recognition for staff creating innovations. This type of group is more difficult to turn around. When Bill Crouse took over ODSI, an ailing medical diagnostics company (nine presidents in 10 years!), he turned many of these profiles into triple greens.[5] How? He attacked the areas that drove the cynicism and demonstrated by action that the company needed to leverage its talent more effectively by improving person-job fit and technology, by communicating more openly, and by showing that those who step up to the new challenges will experience career growth. Many talented people began to sign on to the "new deal," allowing Bill's team to post never-before growth and innovative product introductions within 24 months.

Each of the eight profiles helps the management team and the HR specialists target resources more effectively to enable the manager of that unit to succeed. Different profiles often call for different interventions—coaching, training, resources, varied information, adjusted policies—that move the people of this profile to triple greens.

One major side benefit of the ACE thinking and these profiles is in helping managers become better leaders. Many managers are promoted because of their technical, sales, or other skills, and yet as they take on increased responsibility, the relational and people skills make or break careers. These ACE profiles can help managers close their blind spots. In subsequent chapters, we will discuss more about the measurement of ACE and how you can create such profiles.

Action Tips

In this chapter we have demonstrated that three key factors govern optimal investment returns on human capital: Alignment, Capabilities, and Engagement, known as People Equity. When measured and managed effectively, these factors are powerful in enabling the organization to execute its overall strategy far more effectively.

Consider the following:

- Do you have a high-level ACE view of your organization? If not, try building one that will give senior leaders a good strategic look at how human capital is being leveraged.
- Does your current employee survey include A, C, and E factors or only Engagement and entitlement items? Managers and executives only buy into employee measures that help them reach their goals more effectively.
- Does your current survey include the drivers of A, C, and E so that managers do not need to go on a fishing trip to discover them through more cumbersome methods?
- How well are your leaders doing with the talent entrusted in them? Are they getting high A, C, and E scores?

Chapter 5

Strategic Employee Surveys: Planning and Design

"The most important part is the upfront work. The organization must be completely clear about what it most wants to know, and that it is something worth fixing. It should be an issue or issues related to business performance. Commitments to act on the results should be made up front, and the survey providers should make this discussion as concrete as possible."

—Howard Winkler, Manager, Southern Company

One of the keys to the success of improvement efforts in the quick-serve restaurant organization described in Chapter 4 was the strategic nature of its employee survey. At the outset of the organization's survey program, interviews with senior managers were used to identify people issues that made a difference to business performance. For example, at the restaurant level, the interviews prompted the design of questions regarding food quality, the equipment used in food preparation, the range of product offerings, and food safety, as well as more standard items on speed and service quality.

When survey follow-up efforts to improve the performance of lower-performing restaurants were undertaken, the time spent identifying issues at the beginning of the survey process enabled the team to quickly pinpoint the most critical issues in each location. The connection to specific business issues is one of the factors that differentiate strategic surveys from more conventional employee surveys.

A strategic employee survey is an indispensable tool for an organization's talent optimization efforts. Strategic surveys focus on the people issues that have the greatest impact on business performance and that provide a road map for priority setting and action planning on crucial aspects of talent management.

When the restaurant organization began the survey process, it, like many organizations, had been conducting employee surveys for years, but people were frustrated with the exercise. And the organization failed to realize the business value that can come from a well-designed and conducted strategic survey.

Most organizations find themselves somewhere along the evolutionary scale of survey development shown in Table 5.1.

A strategic survey has several advantages over more traditional employee surveys:

- Strategic surveys capture the attention of senior management. Their direct linkage to business strategy and business results generates both substantial executive interest in the results and a strong commitment to action on the part of the leadership team.
- Because strategic surveys are directly linked to business results, the survey findings tell management where to invest to add value. Rather than leading to scattered investments in a wide array of tactical programs, these surveys help guide management to the most pressing people issues.
- The results provide early warning signals of impending problems, as strategic people issues are often leading indicators of business performance.

Consider the case of a health care company that specializes in the development and manufacture of several diagnostic products. This company's broad-based survey indicated a number of areas of concern but provided no guidance regarding priorities; the survey offered no way to identify the areas in which action would have the most impact on the business. Frustrated with their survey, and

Table 5.1 Evolution of Employee Surveys

Category	Temperature-Taking Surveys	Employee Entitlement or Employee Relations Surveys	Tactical Issues Surveys	Strategic Surveys
Content	Focuses on issues awareness	Focuses on morale, satisfaction with pay, benefits, job security; and other employee relations issues	Focuses primarily on employee engagement or specific topics such as safety, diversity, or ethics	Focuses on strategy execution and all three human capital components: alignment, capabilities, and engagement and their drivers/enablers
Linkage to Outcomes	No linkage	Limited linkage to employee relations outcomes	Linkage to employee engagement, turnover, and performance	Strong linkage to customers, operations, and business outcomes
Action	Low action	Action frequently aimed at corporate HR initiatives to improve morale, stem turnover, and design benefits	Feedback and action aimed at targeted issues, managerial skills, or HR processes that influence employee engagement	Enterprise and local action aimed at human capital effectiveness and business performance
Management Commitment	Low management commitment	Commitment to action is often low or narrowly focused	Commitment varies across levels and functions; greater emphasis on middle management or unit themes	Strong leadership ownership and action; high middle-management involvement
Resources	Few resources allocated to address issues	Follow-up resources (time and funding) targeted defensively	Follow-up resources targeted tactically	Follow-up resources targeted strategically
Assumptions				
	"It's better to know than not."	"Happy employees are productive employees."	"Surveys help us improve people and people processes."	"Human capital management is a critical strategic challenge."

needing to mobilize their workforce for near-term improvements in both product development and sales, executives refocused their questionnaire, removing excess items on traditional employee satisfaction issues (such as satisfaction with pay, benefits, and working conditions) and adding questions to tap into issues relating to innovation, recognition, training, and sales force tools and deployment, all of which they knew had a direct impact on their ability to achieve strategic objectives.

Their new survey focused the attention of senior team members on several key concerns. As a result of the change, the survey has helped them make targeted improvements in a number of areas, removing barriers to timely product development, improving recognition programs, making changes in sales force management, and implementing management changes in several units. These changes have led to improvements in their strategy execution, sales force productivity, and business growth despite a sluggish economy.

However, the organization must be willing and able to make the commitment required by a strategic survey. Melodee Steeber, Assistant Vice President of Organizational Development at Trustmark Insurance advises, "Have a very candid conversation with your company's senior leadership team to talk about exactly why you are undertaking a survey and what you're looking to accomplish."

Not every executive will be onboard from the beginning. Some will be skeptics. Some may have had negative experiences with past surveys. "Get alignment from the top, right from the beginning. Make sure that influential leaders understand and buy into the research behind the survey and the reason for conducting it," says Alison Brunger, HR Business Partner at Valeant Pharmaceuticals.

If the senior team is not ready for a strategic survey, you may need to start with a more basic approach—a more tactical survey or possibly even just a "temperature taking" effort. The latter can be a starting point if expectations are managed carefully. Conducting a survey leads employees to expect action will be taken on their input. If that is not the case, the limited purpose of the survey must be clearly and carefully explained. Otherwise, there will be a negative impact as expectations go unfulfilled.

Creating a Strategic Survey

How does an organization design and implement a strategic survey? Survey content must be grounded in business strategy throughout the survey process; from design to analysis to implementation, the focus must be kept on the most strategic people issues.

An organization could build its strategic survey from scratch, but it need not do so. Typically some content from a legacy survey may be preserved in a strategic survey, although new issues are likely to be added, and some items in existing areas are likely to be edited or eliminated.

An organization need not move to a full-blown strategic survey in its first effort to focus its survey on people issues with a high level of business impact. We have worked with many organizations that walked before they ran, checking A, C, and E and doing analyses and follow-up work to demonstrate business impact on one or two issues. As success builds on success, a business case can be established that enables development of a more comprehensive strategic survey over time.

The remainder of this chapter will focus on developing strategic survey content and on planning and designing the survey. The two areas are closely linked. Planning and design are the first two phases in a six-phase process, as shown in Figure 5.1. Phases I, II, and III will be covered in this chapter, and other phases will be examined in subsequent chapters.

Defining Survey Content

To truly engage senior leadership with survey results, members of the leadership team must see the connection between taking action on survey issues and improving business results. Over the years, we have seen presentations of survey findings in which the leadership team was truly engaged and others in which they appeared to be going through the motions. Often survey content was the issue. Though management may express empathy with issues related to employee satisfaction and motivation, it needs to see the business impact of the issues to put improvement efforts on its priority list.

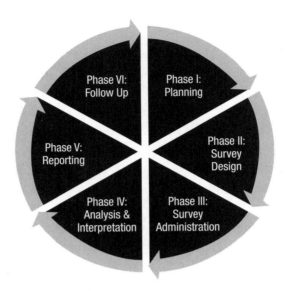

Figure 5.1 The Six Phases of the Survey Process

Trustmark's Steeber advised keeping focused:

> Avoid the temptation to ask too many questions about too
> many topics. There are a lot of questions you may want to ask
> because you might find the responses interesting. Focus on
> those survey items which will give you meaningful data that
> you can connect to your business strategy. Don't ask about
> items which you know you cannot or will not do anything
> about. For example, if there are certain parts of your benefits
> package that you know are absolutely not up for discussion,
> don't even bother asking employees for feedback because you
> will only frustrate people.

We have learned that survey content is best tailored to strategic
people issues—factors required by your workforce to reach strategic
goals. The survey process should begin with a series of questions addressing the key people issues, and the survey should be grounded
in a model that ensures that all the pertinent issues are captured.

Our approach at this point in the process is based on our strategy mapping work, as described in Chapter 2. At the outset of a strategy mapping exercise, leaders are first asked to articulate the strategy and business goals; next they are asked to consider the people, customer, operational, environmental, and financial factors that impact the goals. They then select the few primary factors in each area and map the relationship among these factors. The identification of strategic people or talent issues is one of the outcomes of this process. Many organizations in fact have then extended this thinking to the creation of a talent strategy, where talent is thought about broadly as the knowledge, skills, abilities, experiences, and energy that all people bring to the organization in its pursuit of its goals.

In the development of a strategic employee survey, understanding the overall business and talent strategies helps focus the areas of measurement on principal business drivers (people and process) that employees will be able to rate. Whereas traditional employee surveys often focus on employee motivation, commitment, and related drivers, strategic surveys go beyond these to assess other strategic business drivers. For example, employees often have a strong understanding of customer or supplier issues, the process effectiveness, or even the organizational structure. When two interdependent units have been structurally separated, for example, employees can report on the levels of communication, cooperation, and process effectiveness.

To launch survey development, three questions should be posed to the leadership team in Phase I, at the outset of the survey process:

1. What are the most important business goals for your organization to achieve?
2. What people results (for example, retention of high performers, high engagement levels, alignment with the organization's mission and direction) are critical to achieving organizational goals?
3. What people drivers (for example, strategy communication, leadership, professional development, diversity, per-

formance management) have an impact on performance on these people results?

This line of questioning typically results in identification of a range of issues that can be translated into survey questions. Questionnaire development marks the transition from Phase I of the survey process to Phase II.

For example, a recent client in the utility industry developed a survey that included a set of custom questions on a company-wide effort to communicate and embed its strategic business model, and a company in a retail business included a module designed to assess the extent to which it was living by the elements in its corporate values statement.

Organizations will vary in their custom items, such as the items on food products and services used in the restaurant organization, but a core set of strategic people issues typically emerges in this process.

We have found that most of these issues can be captured in the People Equity framework defined in Chapter 4. As noted there, the Metrus Institute has performed a substantial amount of research to document the relationship of the three key People Equity factors to business outcomes. To reiterate, the three factors are:

- Alignment—Are all employees rowing in the same direction and synchronized across different interdependent teams?
- Capabilities—Do employees have the skills, information, and resources to meet customer expectations?
- Engagement—Are employees not only satisfied but also committed, energetic advocates for their organization?

These three factors serve as a productive way to frame management's answers to the second question in Phase I of the process, "What people results are critical to achieving organizational goals?"

Answers to question 3, "What people drivers have an impact on performance on these people results?", can typically be classified into the five drivers and four enablers of People Equity, as defined in Chapter 4.

The drivers are the following:

- Talent systems, including such processes as talent acquisition and development, performance management, and recognition and reward
- Technology and business processes, including operating effectiveness, business process improvement and effectiveness, adequacy of tools and technical resources, and effectiveness of knowledge management and information use
- Innovation, including production and use of ideas, creativity, and adaptability
- Structure, including deployment of staff and cross-functional information flow
- Strategy elements unique to the organization

The enablers are the following:

- Supervision, including people, technical, coaching, and communication skills and practices of immediate managers
- Leadership, including confidence in senior management and its ability to set, guide, and create a passion for the organization's direction
- Strategic direction, including clarity of direction and presence of a strategic measurement system
- Values, including such areas as respect, diversity and inclusion, ethical behavior, and teamwork

Note that the People Equity model is a framework for categorizing people issues. In any given organization, some issues may require more attention than others, and some other issues not directly reflected in the model may turn out to be of strategic importance. In general, though, a combination of People Equity and company-specific strategy issues will provide a solid foundation on which to build a strategic survey questionnaire.

A full strategic questionnaire may include about 40 to 50 items, but a high-level representation of the People Equity model can be captured in fewer than 20. The goal is to generate content specific enough to identify the organization's leading strengths and concerns without getting bogged down with excessive detail. The details and specific direction for action are best fleshed out in the implementation phase, as described later in Chapter 7.

The Survey Process

Posing the three Phase I questions to senior management is a key aspect of the planning phase. In addition to defining content for the survey, the process of asking these questions, whether in a group session or in a series of one-on-one interviews, helps raise awareness of the business focus of the survey and helps secure the leadership team's buy-in to the process and the survey results. If management has articulated its belief about the relationship between survey issues and business performance, it will be eager to see the findings and to consider action. A parallel process follows with employees, with the same objectives: defining content and securing buy-in. There is a marked difference between the planning phase of a strategic survey and the planning process in other surveys. This difference is part of the essence of a strategic survey: A strategic survey is a *top-down* intervention that starts with the identification of strategic business issues and proceeds to identify the people issues that have the greatest impact on business performance. It is not a *bottom-up* process in which employees articulate the people issues of most concern to them, whether or not they are linked to business performance. The bottom-up approach is more likely to result in an entitlement survey than in a strategic survey.

The good news is that both senior management and employees will articulate a high level of convergence on issues, if the right questions are asked in an effectively moderated discussion. Employees want to be part of a successful enterprise and will be far more engaged if they see a connection between what they do and the achievement of business goals.

Given this approach, the line of inquiry with employees in focus groups conducted at the outset of the survey process should include the following questions:

- What do you believe to be the organization's strategy and its business objectives?
- Do you believe that employees generally buy in to the strategy?
- Do you understand how the work of your department and your own work contribute to the company's achievement of its business objectives?
- Does your unit have the resources and talent needed to meet customer requirements? If not, what are the gaps?

After these issues are defined, discussion can turn to the people drivers and enablers such as leadership, supervision, talent systems, technology, and values. In today's business world, employee focus groups at this phase of the survey are used less often than they were in the past. They are used most often in first-time surveys or when the design of a questionnaire is undergoing a major overhaul. Otherwise, employee focus groups are used more often in Phase VI as part of the survey follow-up process to elicit employees' perspectives on high-priority issues for action as identified in the survey findings.

Today's focus groups need not be conducted in person. Using tools that are readily available for connecting people online, a moderator can conduct an effective focus group with employees. This approach adds the possibility of conducting a session across widely dispersed locations without incurring travel costs.

When positioned effectively, a focus group session engages employees in a discussion of strategy and the people issues connected to it, signaling a different focus for the employee survey, and it provides additional information to guide the development of custom survey questions related to the organization's strategy. Employees live with issues that affect customer relations and operating effectiveness on a day-to-day basis and are eager to participate in a process that is likely to result in improvements on these issues.

That said, though, the organization must deliver on the expectations set by the process. Once the issues have been defined, and once a questionnaire has been constructed to assess the organization's performance on the issues, effective follow-up is imperative.

Analyses must be conducted to identify the issues most in need of attention, and a follow-up program must be launched that attacks these issues head on. These factors are the focus of the next two chapters.

In Phase III (see Figure 5.1), data gathering, the chief consideration is protecting respondent confidentiality to help employees feel comfortable providing their feedback. Many organizations today ask employees to sign in to the survey using personal identification numbers, so their responses can be linked to employee databases and to business outcomes. (Linkage and segmentation will be considered in depth in subsequent chapters). We have found that employees will respond candidly to a survey in which they identify themselves, provided assurances are given that no information will be released to the organization that identifies any individual. This is one reason why many organizations opt to use an outside provider to administer their surveys.

Most organizations today collect survey data electronically, although paper surveys are still used in units where computer access is limited. Because the cost of electronic data gathering is not sensitive to the number of employees, there is no cost reason to sample rather than to take a census of employees. Occasionally, organizations use sampling on pulse surveys, but for the most part a census is preferred. With all employees offered the opportunity to participate, no one will feel excluded, and the organization will have the capability to drill down the analysis of findings to small units.

Given the rapidity of change in organizations today, surveying employees annually is advised. Many organizations go beyond this, using quarterly pulse surveys on selected issues, targeted follow-up surveys to attain feedback on change initiatives, and the like.

Action Tips

1. Work with senior management at the outset of the survey process to identify the people issues that have the greatest impact on business performance. This approach will engage management with the survey process and will enhance management's interest in the results.

2. The three questions (what is your strategy, what do you need from your people to achieve your objectives, and what do you need to do to enable your people to deliver) may be asked one-on-one or as part of a group session. Ideally, a strategy map would result from this exercise, but in the first rounds of moving your survey in a more strategic direction, articulation of issues by individual managers will provide a firm foundation for writing survey items.

3. If you are transforming an existing survey, supplement the old core items with questions that ensure that Alignment, Capabilities, and Engagement are covered. Most likely you will have some items on each issue in your existing questionnaire; typically coverage of Capabilities will be weakest in a more traditional survey.

4. Add custom items on specific business issues. These will help focus attention and action planning when the results are rolled out.

5. Think about the kind of resources you will need to support the survey effort. If you do not have survey content and item writing talent internally, consider bringing in external experts for all or part of the process. Though recent electronic survey tools make conducting surveys easier, more often than not, we have seen organizations writing poor or inappropriate questions (leading, double barreled, fragmented, not actionable), resulting in a loss of credibility to those who manage the process.

6. Less is more if you focus on the right things. Stop and ask yourself whether additional items will truly add value beyond those already included.

7. A major issue for most employees is confidentiality, which is why most organizations use an external vendor to provide third-party protection of the information. With recent privacy laws and confusion between anonymity and confidentiality, experts should be consulted to confirm that your survey does not lead to mistrust, denial of issues, inaction, and refusal to participate in the future.

Chapter 6

Strategic Employee Surveys: Turning Data into Insights

"The last few decades have belonged to a certain kind of person with a certain kind of mind—computer programmers who could crank code, lawyers who could craft contracts, MBAs who could crunch numbers. But the keys of the kingdom are changing hands. The future belongs to a very different kind of person with a very different kind of mind—creators and empathizers, pattern recognizers and meaning makers . . . storytellers."[1]

—Daniel H. Pink, author and journalist

The process of turning data into insights begins long before you have any data. Delivering results in a way that will be meaningful to organization leaders and that will have an impact on business performance means putting the results in the context of the strategic issues facing the organization. This rule applies whether the results are being shared with senior management, managers, or employees. The specific information shared will differ between groups, but the context should be constant. Having a clear understanding of the strategic direction, the value proposition to customers, and the business goals that must be met to deliver that value is a necessary prerequisite to properly interpreting the information you have gathered.

This chapter will focus our discussion on the delivery of the most ubiquitous of organizational assessments: the employee survey. The recommendations, however, are applicable to any organizational survey, audit, or assessment. The actions described in this section occur in phases IV and V of the survey process, as shown in Figure 5.1.

Strategic Analysis for Senior Management

Anyone with a computer and software package can perform sophisticated statistical analyses and assemble impressive (if opaque) presentations. Unfortunately, advanced analytics alone are unlikely to make a lasting impression on senior management. The story has to be told . . . as a story, one with themes built on issues relevant to the organization—themes directly connected to strategic objectives and easily linked to business results. The plot is a detective story, with clues revealed and significant "aha!" moments. The mechanism for advancing the plot is the uncovering of relevant facts from the general to the more specific and illuminating the connections between them.

One of the quickest ways to attract the senior team's attention is to show the story in a single view of the organization that simultaneously illustrates the big picture and some critical details. For organizations using the People Equity model, we have found an ACE Scorecard™ to be a powerful tool. In Figure 6.1, we show an example of an ACE Scorecard™ that summarizes the levels of Alignment, Capabilities, and Engagement (A, C, and E) across major units. Using red, yellow, green color coding (here represented by black, gray, and white), patterns within the organizational structure become clear immediately. Both high-performing units and groups that are struggling are identifiable. Consistent themes such as misalignment in the Sales division and strong Capabilities in Corporate Services are also easily observed.

In a single, clear yet data-rich display like an ACE Scorecard™, several of the most important insights for senior management may be achieved. For example, how much variation in workforce Alignment, Capabilities, and Engagement exists in the organization, and what is the impact? In this example, we can see that Sales has much less favorable results than the other divisions. However, though Alignment is a consistent challenge within the Sales force, the overall negative results are primarily driven by the very low scores in North America. Conversely, in the Support group, results overall are quite favorable. But within the division, Supply Chain displays an atypical pattern. In that unit, Engagement is as high as anywhere else in the division, but Alignment and Capabilities are much lower.

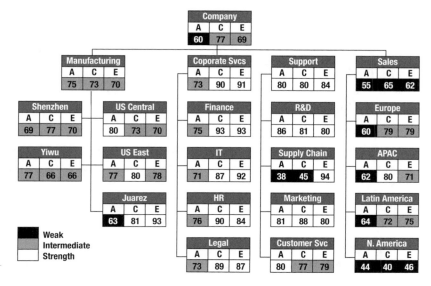

Figure 6.1

Note how we must be careful with aggregated information. When we first look at Sales, we might conclude serious problems exist throughout that organization. However, when we drill down to specific subgroups, we see a good deal of variation across those groups.

In the organization from which these results are taken, Supply Chain was a group with a manager who spent a lot of time "shielding" the team from corporate directives that he did not agree with. Although employees felt secure and supported by their manager and peers, they could see that they were not consistently meeting expectations of their stakeholders—thus the low score on Capabilities. And it was painfully obvious that the team was not aligned with the rest of the company. When your own manager tells you, "This is what the big shots want, but we are going to do it my way," the misalignment cannot be much more evident.

At this point in the story, several key facts have been uncovered in the connection between what is happening at the unit level and what is happening at the division and corporate level. A theme of misalignment has been revealed, with examples both local (Supply Chain) and global (Sales). The ACE Scorecard™ allows leaders to visualize patterns and variations across units. Further analysis of the drivers and enablers of ACE (we recommend measuring them in the survey as well) can detect whether the low Alignment scores in two different units have the same cause. This analysis enables the organization to find common root cause problems that are best addressed collectively. For example, if the A scores are low in many areas, and further examination of the drivers and enablers indicates poor understanding of the company direction and strategy, leaders can embark on a stronger communications strategy to reduce that gap, thereby improving alignment organization-wide. If one area has low Alignment because of fuzzy goals or direction, that gap can be treated directly and differently from the gap in the unit where linkage to rewards is setting off the Alignment alarm bells. The same can be said for Capabilities or Engagement.

When the low A, C, and E scores are varied across units, the organization can deploy its scarce resources in a targeted fashion to spot and treat issues. "The red/yellow/green analysis modeled on an organization chart is a great visual way to see where you are and where you want to go," says Nora Swimm, VP, HR and Corporate Client Services at PJM Interconnection. Donna Hirsch, VP, Organizational Development at Trustmark advises, "Be sure that you break the results down into meaningful groupings. If the units are too large—too high level—the law of averages will conceal any opportunities."

Driver Analysis—Understanding
What Issues Have the Most Impact

Understanding what drives high levels of variation becomes the next step in our analysis. You could spend a lot of time looking at the differences across individual survey items and trying to spot patterns. A better approach is to apply advanced analytics to develop a model of the key drivers for Alignment, Capabilities, and Engagement. Excellent techniques are available to help pinpoint the drivers of major issues, such as high turnover or low engagement.[2] The results of these driver analyses can be a powerful tool for prioritizing opportunities and identifying points of leverage to improve the organization.

Driver analyses usually proceed in two phases. The first phase examines the broad categories covered by the survey to determine which have the most impact on, say, Alignment, Capabilities, or Engagement. Figure 6.2 shows the results of a first-stage driver analysis for a particular company. In this example, Growth and Development was identified as a powerful driver of Engagement but was relatively unimportant as a driver of Alignment. Strategy and Direction was the powerful driver of Alignment. Performance Management, on the other hand, was a strong driver of Alignment, Capabilities, *and* Engagement. The relative importance of the drivers is shown as the percentage of variance explained (or "driven") by the driver. For example, under Engagement we see that in this company the Growth and Development driver explains 27 percent of overall Engagement—almost four times as much as the Senior Management driver (7 percent). Improvements on growth and development issues will therefore have much more impact on Engagement than improvement on senior management issues.

The second phase of the driver analysis looks within the most compelling survey categories to identify which specific items have the most impact. The example cited above, where Performance Management is a top driver of Alignment, Capabilities, and Engagement, provides a good illustration. Different items within the Performance Management category are most substantial for A, C, and E respectively, as illustrated in Table 6.1. Alignment is most strongly affected by clarity of individual responsibilities and the link between pay and performance; Capabilities is most strongly affected by the extent to which performance reviews help employees improve their performance and accountability, whereas Engagement is most strongly affected by the extent to which the Performance Management system recognizes outstanding work, meaningful recognition, and the performance-pay link.

In large organizations, driver analyses can be done for each business unit or for different regions. For one global financial services organization, we contrasted the relative importance of a group of drivers for Engagement. The differences between regions were

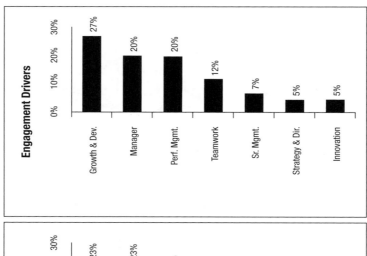

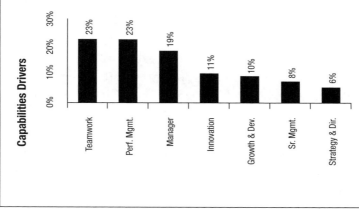

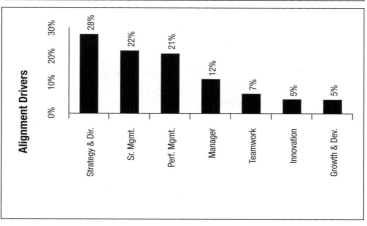

Figure 6.2 Driver Importance Varies by ACE Factor

Table 6.1 Phase 2 Driver Analysis Identifies Key Points of Leverage

Performance Management Issues	Strong driver of		
	Alignment	Capabilities	Engagement
Performance reviews help improve performance.		●	
People know what is expected of them.	●		
The performance management system recognizes outstanding work.			●
Timely positive feedback.			●
Pay/performance link.	●		●
Equitable performance.		●	

enlightening. In the established and stable North American region, professional growth, diversity and inclusion, and ethics were the top three drivers of Engagement. In the Asia-Pacific region the top three drivers of Engagement were completely different: change management, senior management (communication and behaviors), and work/life balance.

In the Asia-Pacific region, the organization was going through extremely rapid growth and multiple reorganizations and was challenged to find and attract sufficient talent. As a result, Asia-Pacific employees experienced a different organization compared to those in North America. For senior managers with global responsibility, this information was invaluable as they designed and implemented follow-up strategies to the survey.

Practical Analysis for Managers

The other audience for survey results is the actual end-user group: managers. Although executives need a strategic perspective in the information presented to them, managers need a tool that helps them quickly and easily identify their primary opportunities. Simplicity and clarity are essential. Charts are more effective than dense tables of numbers. Percentages are preferred over mean scores. People have difficulty relating to mean scores; is 3.35 good or bad? On the other hand, managers can directly relate a percentage of employees who gave favorable (or unfavorable) responses. Managers need to move rapidly from data to action, so the information presented to them must facilitate that progression.

Providing an overall profile for the unit allows a manager to swiftly gain a sense of the team's state. Profiles such as those detailed in Figure 6.1 are useful because they remind managers of the "big picture" for the unit. Most surveys contain far too many questions and can easily bury a manager in extraneous detail. A profile or unit-specific scorecard acts as a check on that tendency and provides a concise and intuitive summary.

Extracting key opportunities and summarizing them for the manager in a list format is helpful. Though some managers will spend time poring over the full report for their group, whenever possible it is beneficial to provide efficiencies that shortcut needless analysis and frustration on the part of the manager. After all, they are not organizational psychologists; they are managers looking for easily interpretable information they can put to work. An ideal approach is to apply a logic algorithm that takes into account several aspects of the results and combines them to identify top opportunities. For example, we have had success with an algorithm that mathematically combines four distinct factors to rank-order each survey item as a potential opportunity. The top 10 opportunities are identified for each manager. Those opportunities can then be prioritized by the manager in collaboration with team members, selecting two or three areas for action.

Identifying the opportunities should be more than just rank-ordering items based on how favorable the responses are. The standard top 10 list of the least favorable items is much too simplistic. In fact there are four basic criteria for opportunity identification:

1. Is the item one of the least favorable or most unfavorable in the report? Ideally, any approach should consider both the proportion of favorable responses and the proportion of unfavorable responses (keeping in mind that a large proportion of neutral responses is possible).
2. How much has a score changed since the last survey? A low score moving in the right direction may be less of a priority than a slightly higher score dropping quickly.

3. On what issues is the unit substantially less favorable than the company (or division) as a whole? Is that the result of a known situation?

4. How do the results compare to external benchmarks? When available, normative data can help put results in context. For example, some issues (like questions about compensation) rarely score more than 50 to 60 percent favorable in any organization.

Prioritizing for Action

A report, even one that uses an automated algorithm based on the criteria above, can only go so far in helping a manager prioritize. How does a manager choose a small number of priorities from a list of opportunities? A number of factors must be considered when selecting priorities for action. In addition to the criteria used in the identifying opportunities, think through these questions:

- Is the issue something over which you have local control?
- Are there issues that closely relate to strategic imperatives for the company or for your unit?
- Would some issues have more impact on your unit's performance than others?
- Are some issues likely to be important to a large percentage of your unit's employees?
- If a driver analysis is available, which items have been identified as having the most impact on ACE and other leading outcomes in your organization?
- What is your team's perspective? When reviewing the results with them, you may find they have a clear sense of what is most urgent.

In short, results for managers should use basic frequency (percentage) data displays, rely mostly on charts, and proactively identify the biggest opportunities for improvement. The results should also be packaged in a way that clearly ties them back to the strategic and business issues identified on the front end of the survey process.

New Perspectives on Survey Data:
Getting Beyond the Basics

Key insights can be obtained by looking at survey data from perspectives that simply have not always been available. Many organizational surveys today are confidential, but not anonymous. The survey administrator no longer gathers answers to demographic questions, but connects responses instantaneously to a database derived from the company's own HR systems. This technique results in more complete and more accurate demographic information on the survey respondents. It also enables incredible flexibility in analysis and reporting. Any variable available to the company now has the potential to be used for generating new insights and perspectives. Previously, comparing high-potential employees to others would never have been possible, because there was no way to identify them within the data. By using a confidential, unique identifier, survey responses can be connected to other data. It is even possible to merge post-survey turnover information and develop models that can predict who is at risk of leaving based on his or her survey responses.

Analysis of High-Potential Employees

Most organizations have identified a subset of employees who are considered high potential. They are built into succession plans and are often given special assignments to help them further develop their potential. Retaining and developing these individuals is critical to the company's future success, and in many cases the company may already depend much more on this group than on other employees.

Being aware of the issues specific to this group and how its members may differ from other employees can be a powerful advantage for the organization. Because competition for the best employees is fierce in any labor market, a deep understanding of the high-potential group can ensure that the company is striking the right balance in providing challenges, development, and recognition.

In one organization we examined the attitudes of the high-potential employees, including their perceptions of work/life balance and the average length of their workweek (see Figure 6.3). In general, the high potentials were among the most engaged employees in the company. But each year the survey was conducted, they reported working more hours and becoming less satisfied with their work/life balance. They were also increasingly frustrated with management of poor performers and some aspects of Capabilities, such as technology resources. As a result, whereas ACE scores for the company were trending up overall, the scores for the high-potential group were declining.

When confronted with the data, senior management acknowledged that these individuals were not being given additional projects for developmental reasons but because they were the ones whom the organization knew it could count on. Their reward for stepping up to the plate was to have more work piled on. In response to the findings, a formal approach was devised to identify developmental projects and to make certain that the "extra" activities were chosen for the benefit of both the high-potential employee and the company. In addition, refinements were made to the performance management system to better differentiate between strong and weak performers. One year later, the downward slide had stopped (and reversed on many issues), and the ever-expanding workweek had stabilized.

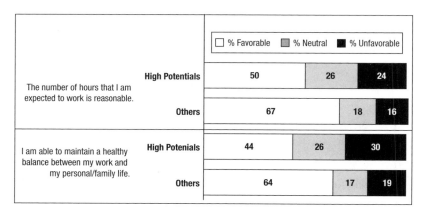

Figure 6.3 High-Potential Employees Compared to Others

Analysis of Performance Levels

A similar analysis can be done by integrating performance evaluation data with the survey data, making the comparison of results from top, middle, and poor performers possible. It is not unusual to find that poor performers have more negative attitudes toward the performance management process, and in general, less favorable views of the organization. In fact, the most common pattern observed is that better-performing employees are more favorable in their responses to survey questions. A retail banking organization was deeply concerned when survey results indicated that the highest-rated employees gave the least favorable ratings. They were highly aligned but very low on Capabilities and Engagement.

The organization had little turnover, and the average tenure was quite long. When employees' performance lagged, there was little consequence. Even though top performers were recognized and received greater merit pay increases, they were a frustrated group. Maintaining a high degree of motivation is difficult when you observe your co-workers simply coasting. As with the organization that analyzed its high-potential group, these findings served as an early warning flag for senior management.

Priority Matrix

A useful tool that will aid decisions is the priority matrix. For each issue addressed in the survey, a measure of performance is charted against an indicator of importance. For example, when managers and employees are asked to give feedback on the level of internal service provided by departments such as Human Resources and IT, a priority plot can help identify strengths and opportunities. A subtle but informative refinement is the bubble chart. A bubble chart effectively displays results in three dimensions.

In the example shown in Figure 6.4, importance is shown on the vertical axis and performance on the horizontal axis. The size of the bubble representing each data point can represent a third variable. In this case, the size of the bubble indicates the level of familiarity

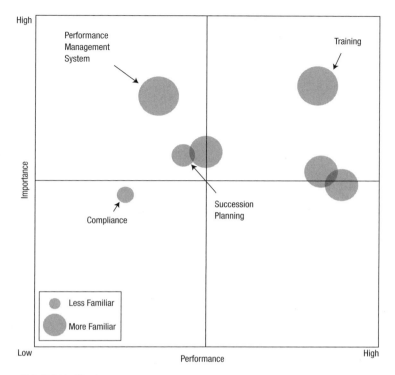

Figure 6.4 Bubble Chart

or understanding that respondents report regarding each function listed on the survey. Figure 6.4 illustrates that Human Resources' compliance function is of moderate importance and is not rated highly. Yet the small diameter of the bubble indicates that the department's stakeholders may not have a full understanding of everything Human Resources does in the compliance arena. The appropriate response may be increased communication or education before undertaking any process improvement initiatives.

Linkage Analysis: Analyzing Impact

Advanced analytics and innovative analyses can lead us to many valuable insights about people issues in the organization. But in the end they all describe the "what," and senior management will always ask

"So what?" The best approach to "so what" is linkage analysis. In linkage analysis, we determine the real impact on business performance of the measures we have gathered. For example, just how much difference does it make if Alignment, Capabilities, and Engagement are high?

Linkage analysis is particularly powerful in settings with many similar units. Whenever a large number of similar units have easily tracked financial, customer, and human capital metrics, the potential for linkage analysis is significant. In one large regional retail organization, we examined the ability of ACE to explain the difference in sales, profits, turnover, and customer satisfaction. The results provided a clear signpost for the organization to maximize business performance across many locations.

ACE could explain half of the variance in turnover between locations. In fact, the top quartile of locations averaged 20 percent less turnover, which translated to seven fewer new hires per month. Less time spent interviewing and hiring meant managers could spend more time coaching current employees and focusing on operations. Those top locations also averaged 10 percent higher sales and 30 percent higher profits compared to the bottom quartile. High ACE scores also led directly to greater customer satisfaction, and when customers did complain, complaints were almost twice as likely to be successfully resolved.

Linkage analysis can also be used in nonretail settings. All that is required is a uniform way to measure business performance across units. A simple way to create a uniform measure across disparate business units is to track their success rate in meeting their annual goals or targets. A large southern utility that uses the ACE model has found that, across different business units each with separate goals, a clear pattern emerges. Those business units in the top quartile for ACE consistently achieve 90 percent or more of their annual goals. The bottom two quartiles generally achieve only 20 percent of their goals.

For the C-suite, linkage analysis demonstrates the business relevance of an employee survey. It reminds them that the survey is a management tool to help the organization succeed. The days of such assessments being "something that human resources does to keep people happy" are long gone. Today, employee surveys are only justified if they can help the organization reach its strategic objectives and deliver value for its stakeholders.

Action Tips

1. Take time to identify priorities, and be willing to go wherever the data take you.

2. Consider having executives "predict" key findings before the survey. Review the predictions before sharing actual results. The extent to which predictions are similar says a lot about the Alignment of the leaders. The fact that there will be (almost always) some hits and many misses will help leaders see the value of the survey because it cannot be dismissed as something "we already knew the answer to."

3. When presenting results, particularly for senior teams, consider the group's point of view: What is the context that will make the information most relevant for group members? Are details appreciated, or is there little tolerance for them? Are they used to high-level reviews, or are they accustomed to looking at unit-by-unit findings?

Chapter 7

Strategic Employee Surveys: Turning Insight into Business Results

"The ACE model helped us understand where our gaps were, but we had to take the right actions to achieve performance impact. Since we began taking those actions three years ago, we have experienced a 29 percent improvement in ACE scores."

—Terry Boston, President and CEO, PJM Interconnection

An effective survey follow-up effort can result in dramatic change, as seen recently at one employee benefits company, Trustmark. Melodee Steeber, Assistant Vice President of Organizational Development at Trustmark noted:

> I saw one of our business units go from being in the bottom three scores in the company to being in the top three scores in the company in about 18 months. This business unit had gone through a significant amount of change, including layoffs. The business unit leader knew things weren't great, but she didn't realize how bad it was until they got the results of their employee engagement survey. This group immediately conducted focus groups with all employees to get more information regarding what needed to change, formed teams of employees and managers to work on different aspects, and prioritized action items. Their hard work paid off in the improved subsequent survey results.

Concerted effort is required to effect change. Many C-suite ex-ecutives have told us that even with a good questionnaire, decent analysis, and valid findings, they are not realizing the needed im-provements in employee engagement, retention of top performers, or higher customer or financial performance following the survey. Why do organizations fail to obtain impact from their survey results? One restaurant group described in earlier chapters had an enlighten-ing insight: One-size-fits-all solutions could not be used to secure the desired impact. Company executives saw that their Alignment, Capabilities, and Engagement profiles varied from restaurant to res-taurant and that the drivers of ACE—performance management, lead-ership, and communications, for example—also differed.

Armed with this information, management implemented follow-up action-planning efforts tailored to the specific profiles of their low-performing restaurants and was able to improve scores in 90 percent of these units within six months.

The organization had developed a strategic survey that addressed the right issues, but that was just the beginning of the follow-up process. Equipped with the results and with a commitment from the leadership team to take action, executives quickly identified the high-priority issues, took steps to make sure that managers had the right skills to lead follow-up actions, fed back the findings, and developed action plans.

A strategic employee survey that includes all the right questions along with an analysis that provides a road map for change can be a powerful tool for business decision making. But the effectiveness of the survey program ultimately depends on the quality of survey follow-up and implementation. The actions examined in this chapter take place in Phase VI of the survey process, as displayed earlier in Figure 5.1.

Many potentially effective survey programs lose momentum at this point in the process, leaving the organization with a highly vis-ible set of people issues that are not being addressed, leaving em-ployees with a higher level of cynicism about management's commit-ment to its people, and leaving actions that could improve business performance on the table. Not taking action on survey results is worse than not having done the survey at all.

To fully realize the potential value of strategic survey follow-up, an organization needs a disciplined process for taking action and a well-prepared cadre of managers with good survey follow-up and implementation skills.

Gaps in these areas can derail an otherwise well-designed and analyzed strategic survey effort. Each area is considered in turn below.

A Disciplined Process for Taking Action

The survey follow-up process can be defined in terms of the seven steps displayed in Figure 7.1.

Before we delve into the seven steps, it is important to consider one of the marked differences between strategic surveys and many other employee surveys: Identification of the priority issues for survey follow-up begins with senior management's consideration of the potential business impact of action. In essence, this difference makes survey follow-up a *top-down* process that is quite different from the *bottom-up* approach to action planning used over the years in many organizations.

Historically, companies that used bottom-up action planning cascaded the survey findings down the organization, with each level reviewing the information that pertained to it. Action plans were developed at the local level and were then sent back up the organization for review. Though the process maximized local involvement and if done effectively led to action on local problems, it required that recommendations be passed up the organization in areas that needed higher levels of authority to resolve.

This process succeeded in creating buy-in from employees and from many managers when executed well, but it has declined in use and effectiveness over the past decade for a number of reasons. First, the focus was often employee satisfaction, and the mindset was often one of entitlement. Senior leaders soon became wary of the employee survey as a tool that simply increased the length of its to-do list, often with little impact on their ability to reach their goals or to enhance organizational performance.

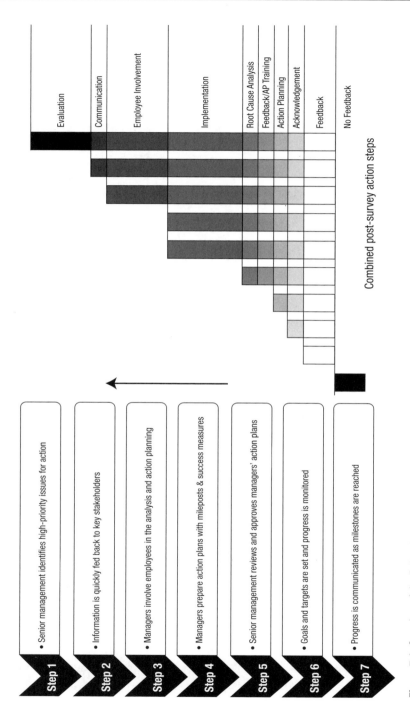

Figure 7.1 Overview of the Follow-Up Process

Second, the process was cumbersome and time consuming and not well suited to the current era of intense competitive pressure, ever-increasing speed, sharp focus, and agility.

Third, there is no guarantee that the issues identified by the process will have business impact; historically, the approach produced too much bottom-up information that cluttered the strategic picture. Although some of that information was essential to building organizational health and dealing with dominant issues, in today's fast-paced, information-clogged environment, information focused on strategic people issues provides more value. This approach requires top-down prioritization of the issues that are most strategic, coupled with rapid feedback from the workforce.

A senior HR executive in the technology industry observed,

> "Avoid making things too complicated, especially for line managers. Our survey reporting is tailored to deliver meaningful, actionable results to the right audience. Avoid bombarding your line managers with too much data that prevents them from responding. One or two completed actions mean more to employees than a well-intended 20 item action plan that is never shared."

Let's now take a look at the critical steps in the action planning process, as displayed in Figure 7.1.

Step 1: Senior management identifies high-priority issues for follow-up action.

Delivery of results from a traditional employee survey can leave management with a laundry list of issues and no way to set priorities for action. In contrast, when the results of a strategic survey are delivered to the leadership team, several assets are in place to help focus attention on the main issues for follow-up. These assets include the following:

- *Strategic context.* At the beginning of the strategic survey process, management is asked to respond to the three questions posed at the beginning of the survey process, as noted in Chapter 5. The questions are:

o   What are the most important business goals for your organization to achieve?

o   What people results are critical for the organization if it is to achieve these goals?

o   What people drivers (for example, communication of strategy, leadership, professional development, diversity, performance management) have an impact on performance on these people results?

In a strategic survey the answers to these questions are used to guide development of survey items, so management will have a business context for examining the results and identifying performance gaps on items that they know have an impact on business performance. The process of articulating these issues will also enhance management's interest in the results, as managers will want to know the state of the company on issues that they have defined as important.

Depending on the organization, the answers to these questions may have been used as a foundation for building a talent strategy map. If not, they still provide strategic content and serve to pique senior management interest in the findings.

- *Analytical indicators.* The results of driver and linkage analyses that demonstrate empirically how specific items or clusters of items affect business outcomes such as retention of top employees, customer relations, and financial performance will help identify action issues. For example, as noted in Chapter 6, where these issues were explored in depth, an analysis in one company revealed that its performance management system had a strong impact on employee views of Alignment, Capabilities, and Engagement.

Those who have been through a more traditional survey follow-up process may ask whether the top-down approach to identifying issues risks missing pressing people issues. In the authors' experience, the answer is almost always "no" for the following reasons:

1. From the outset of the survey process, every effort will have been taken to incorporate the people issues that make the greatest difference in business performance.
2. Linkage and driver analyses will detect the issues most likely to affect performance.
3. The root cause analysis process used in follow-up sessions will surface underlying causes of problems, whether or not these have been the subject of particular survey items. At this point in the survey process, the results become a springboard for discussion of the central issues and the actions required to address them. If a burning issue has somehow been missed in the questionnaire, it will undoubtedly surface when discussing the causes of problems and developing the actions to address them.

Even with these tools, management will most likely need to make some choices for follow-up action. For example, the results of a strategic survey for a client in a service business revealed concerns in four areas: trust in communications from the leadership team, the climate for innovation, work/life balance, and recognition for exceptional performance. From the analysis, these concerns emerged as drivers of overall Engagement and Capabilities in the organization.

As the leadership team explored these issues, it realized that a people-resources issue cutting across several areas of the survey was at the core of many of its concerns. A recent staff reduction had not appeared to have been performed strategically. As a result, trust levels were lowered; willingness to take the risks required for innovation had been diminished; people felt stressed and overworked; and little attention seemed to be paid to the difference between good and poor performers when reductions were made.

Management elected to address the people-resources issue directly, believing that it was the correct starting point for addressing what the analyses and their discussions demonstrated were concerns in the areas of trust, innovation, balance, and recognition.

Step 2: Information on these issues is quickly fed back to key stakeholders for discussion and input.

Note that the process of issue identification described in Step 1 does not and should not preclude candid and balanced feedback of survey results. Quick presentation of the overall survey results in town hall meetings, company publications, or other appropriate forums should be used to inform employees of the results and to describe the process to be used to address key issues. Action items need not be identified at this point, although when they have been identified, they should be communicated to the workforce along with a reminder of the process to be used to address the issues.

Timely and candid feedback of survey findings, along with a strong management commitment to take action to address concerns emerging from the findings, have long been a hallmark of effective employee surveys. Employees are eager to know the survey results, and they are well aware if the feedback does not provide a well-balanced overview of strengths and concerns. Employees also expect that some action will be taken to address concerns expressed. As Nora Swimm, Vice President of HR and Corporate Client Services at PJM Interconnection, noted, "Our structured follow up to the survey helped us improve employee alignment, capability, and engagement. Our overall score improved because we used the feedback on where enterprise wide support was needed and what was needed at the department levels."

But these factors have been recognized by survey practitioners for many years; they are not unique to strategic employee surveys. Strategic surveys are differentiated from other surveys at this point in both the way priorities are set and the way the follow-up process is driven based on these priorities.

Step 3: Involvement of employees is critical at this stage, whether organizational or departmental issues are being examined.

The issues identified for action in a strategic survey are people issues that have been defined top down by management, not bottom up by employees in workgroups. Employees bring their day-to-day experience to the process of developing an understanding of the issues and devising solutions to address them. As noted in Chapter 5, group sessions with employees can be conducted online as well as in person. The online approach enables the organization to employ cross-location task forces to address key issues.

Depending on the issues and the organization, stakeholder groups at this phase of the process can be intact departments, cross-functional task forces, or existing teams already assembled to address business issues (for example, quality or performance improvement teams). If the groups are intact units, such as departments, feedback sessions can be used to address local issues of interest, once again with a focus on the people issues most closely related to business performance. Typically, the teams' first priority will be to address the issues that senior management has asked them to review. If high-priority local issues go beyond these concerns, time can be allocated to address them.

Recall the case of the global consulting firm discussed in Chapter 4. Its survey results revealed that alignment was an issue that warranted focus company-wide, and it identified several HR systems, including aspects of the performance management, reward, and recognition systems, that were drivers of Alignment. A drill down to units revealed that performance levels on these drivers varied substantially, leading the organization to employ custom-tailored action planning programs at the unit level to address the local concerns and in turn to influence alignment issues company-wide.

Step 4: Management prepares action plans to address the issues.

The development of action plans at both the organization-wide and local levels involves the process of root cause analysis. Addressing these causes is likely to have a positive impact on key outcomes. Of course, root cause analysis can be used in more traditional surveys as well. The difference in strategic surveys is the starting point, which is senior management's effort to understand and address a few people issues that have been identified as critical to reaching strategic objectives.

Step 5: Results from the teams' sessions are fed back to the leadership team.

This step assimilates the information, conducts its own analyses, and develops and implements action plans. Once again, the action plan is driven from the top of the organization, with local results carefully considered and examined, but with strategic people issues ultimately dictating the issues selected for action.

Step 6: Goals and targets are set, and progress is monitored.

Having invested the time and resources needed to develop and implement action plans, many organizations believe they are finished with the survey. When this happens, they fall short in achieving organizational improvements from their survey effort. Goal setting and impact evaluation must not be overlooked.

Organizations may be tempted to accept anecdotal evidence as a measure of the success of their efforts, whether these are survey related or not, but disciplined implementation requires effective target setting and impact evaluation. Although the results of next year's survey will shed some light on the effectiveness of action, the information may come too late to make necessary course corrections. Most interventions designed to address people issues should begin to demonstrate an impact within a few months, so tools are needed for near-term assessment of results.

A pulse survey can be useful in this regard. If the intervention is expected to have an effect on issues measured by particular survey items, these items can be incorporated in a survey targeted at the right audience and administered within three to six months. Our experience has shown that most well-targeted improvement areas should start to show change in less than 90 days if actions have been effectively launched and implemented.

Table 7.1 is adapted from a quarterly tracking report for a financial services organization. It shows current scores and annual targets for external customer, internal customer, and employee survey items. Each item appears on a strategy map that also includes financial and operational measures.

Table 7.1 Quarterly Tracking Report for Financial Services Organization

Strategic Performance Measurement Area	Measurement Area	Measurement Tool	Baseline/ Benchmark	Targets	Actual
Internal Value Survey					
Internal Value Survey	Internal Value Survey	Internal Value Survey	Year 1—54% Year 2—62% Year 3—67%	1 yr.—70% 3 yrs.—80%	results expected in last quarter
Client Survey					
Client Satisfaction	Client Satisfaction	Client Survey	Year 1—66% Year 2—72% Year 3—69%	1 yr.—75% 3 yrs.—90%	6mos.—71%
Employee Survey					
Values	Commitment to Client Self-Confidence	Employee Survey	Year 1—62% Year 2—69% Year 3—69%	1 yr.—71% 3 yrs.—85%	results expected in last quarter
Alignment	Clarity Recognition Department goals	Employee Survey	Year 1—49% Year 2—59% Year 3—57%	1 yr.—60% 3 yrs.—75%	results expected in last quarter
Growth/Learning/Innovation	Training Development Change	Employee Survey	Year 1—45% Year 2—54% Year 3—53%	1 yr.—57% 3 yrs.—65%	results expected in last quarter
Leadership	Communication Goals Ethics and Integrity	Employee Survey	Year 1—58% Year 2—69% Year 3—62%	1 yr.—68% 3 yrs.—80%	results expected in last quarter
Engagement	Commitment Intention to stay Company satisfaction	Employee Survey	Year 1—79% Year 2—80% Year 3—77%	1 yr.—80% 3 yrs.—90%	results expected in last quarter

Milestone measures are also useful. Targeted dates for accomplishing tasks along the way to full implementation can be set and monitored.

As improvement on people issues is designed to affect business outcomes, performance on outcome measures can also be used to assess the effectiveness of the improvement efforts. These measures may encompass such areas as employee retention, customer service ratings, operating effectiveness, cost reduction, and profitability improvement.

The survey process, like other tools for business improvement, should demonstrate a return on investment. We have documented a link between both return on assets and return on investment, on the one hand, and effective use of surveys and people measures on the other.[1] For example, organizations in which executives say that their employee surveys provide information valuable in guiding decision making have achieved a 65 percent higher return on investment over a five-year period.

In any case, improvement cannot be taken for granted. The authors have found that the organizations that get the most out of their surveys actively manage evaluation of the follow-up process. They often incorporate action planning evaluation into impact reviews in which they assess performance on major milestones or indicators on regular basis.

Some firms have instituted quarterly surveys that track a limited number of marker items from a baseline survey—either ongoing tracking on core Alignment, Capabilities, and Engagement levels or tracking progress on issues specifically targeted for high-priority action. These surveys provide timely feedback that enables the plan owners to either declare victory or quickly adjust their plan to achieve more effective results.

Organizations that do not conduct pulse surveys with such frequency look for other indicators of performance improvement. These may be surrogate indicators that would be expected to move if the fixes were working. For example, low scores on customer focus that triggered efforts to give more time and attention to customers would be expected to improve customer satisfaction, retention, or buying behavior. Actions in response to low diversity ratings would be expected to reduce complaints or filed actions by minorities or protected classes. The key is looking for the best available indicators that real change has occurred.

Performance gaps in any of the five areas discussed in this chapter can derail an otherwise well-designed and analyzed strategic survey effort. A disciplined approach to all five greatly increases the odds of performance improvement on strategic people issues.

Step 7: As milestones are reached, progress is communicated to the organization.

Communication is vital to keep the organization informed of the issues that emerged from the survey and the commitment of the organization to addressing those concerns. Even when an organization invests in implementing change, it may not get the mileage it could out of the changes by keeping employees informed. Ongoing communications both reinforce the importance of the issues being addressed and remind employees that their input is valued.

Well Prepared Managers with Good Survey Follow-up and Implementation Skills

As noted earlier in this chapter, to fully realize the potential value of strategic survey follow-up, an organization needs a disciplined process for taking action and a well-prepared cadre of managers with good survey follow-up and implementation skills. The process for taking action has just been reviewed. Now, we turn to the preparation of managers for the process.

Preparation of management for follow-up is crucial. An HR manager in the utility industry recommends asking the following questions:

- "How strong is the incumbent supervisory chain of command? Do supervisors see themselves as implementers of change? As representing upper management? If so, things will move along smoothly. If supervisors don't have a clear understanding of what their role is, then change is less likely to result."

- "How effective are Organizational Development staff and resources? Do people need new skills to effect change? If so, are the resources there to train them?"

The effectiveness of the follow-up process, and especially the effectiveness of group sessions designed to feed back survey results and develop action plans, is predicated on the ability of the facilitators to run the sessions. *Most managers will need training to be effective facilitators.*

In the authors' experience, up to 30 percent of managers will find a way to use survey information to effectively address concerns regardless of formal training, whereas 10 percent to 20 percent will have trouble regardless of the training they get. The latter group will inevitably have to be shadowed and supported by outside facilitators. The rest—about half the managers in most organizations—will become substantially better at managing survey follow-up with the right skills.

Most of these skills make up a well-rounded managerial skill set: strategic thinking, business acumen, prioritization and decision making, giving and receiving feedback, knowledge of root cause analysis and other quality tools, team decision making, building effective action plans, and evaluating change. As Trustmark's Melodee Steeber noted,

> "No matter how proficient a manager may or may not be, it is important to ensure that each manager remains accountable for following through on the results. It sends a poor message to employees if responsibility is shifted to another manager who has stronger skills, or to a consultant or the organizational development department."

A requisite set of skills unique to the survey process involves interpreting survey information. Although the other skills should be part of a rounded managerial skill set, we typically find a good deal of variance across them. Many organizations lack the commitment to developing skills in interpreting survey information, which are nothing more than the raw ingredients of effective group problem solving. Most often these skill gaps are simply made relevant and visible during the survey follow-up process.

Training in these areas can take various forms when done in conjunction with the survey process. We have found that focusing on three sets of skills is effective:

- Interpreting the data and prioritizing issues in a strategic framework
- Conducting strategic feedback sessions with employees, identifying root causes and potential solutions, and building strong action plans accepted by both management and employees
- Securing resources, implementing the action plans, and tracking results and impact

Basic skills in these areas can be conveyed in a training session that uses the organization's survey data as the basis for discussion. Ideally each manager should have time to facilitate at least part of the process during the training session, for experience is a far better teacher than observation. Time demands in many organizations dictate that these sessions last only two or three hours. Although three hours will assuredly help, we find that organizations that immerse managers in a full-day training session, where role playing, what-if scenarios, and developing draft action plans are included, build more effective leader skills and stronger improvement plans.

Effective use of manager training is demonstrated by a program run by a 10,000-employee organization. It decided to use a series of follow-up meetings at business unit and department levels to help provide input on two pivotal organization-wide issues identified by the survey: the company's performance management system and the reticence of employees to surface troubling issues. In addition to gathering information to help management develop targeted action plans for the issues, these sessions served to communicate management's intention to examine and address issues that most employees knew would require fundamental culture change. The sessions also provided a forum for managers to work on local issues in their units.

To prepare managers for this effort, the organization conducted a series of three-hour training sessions for managers. Most sessions were run for intact units, and wherever possible group size was kept to 20 participants. After brief remarks by the unit head on the key findings, participants were given a presentation on the fundamentals of the action planning process. Then they were divided into subgroups, each led by a facilitator who simulated the process of root cause analysis and solution development. Managers were then asked to schedule sessions with their employees and to post their recommended actions on a website set up for this purpose. This process enabled the HR representatives to summarize the information across groups and to present recommendations for consideration by senior management.

If you are using a strategic ACE survey, we also recommend that managers who score low in A, C, or E be strongly encouraged to sign up for training modules targeted to their area of development. In as short as one half day, managers typically walk away with new insights about blind spots and ways in which they can improve the lagging performance area.

Why Surveys Fail

Over the course of the last three chapters we have told you what to do to make an employee survey work well. Now we will tell you what can make a survey go wrong and will remind you what steps to take to avoid the potential pitfalls.

Even the best-intentioned survey program can fail to deliver value. Our experience indicates that vulnerability to failure is present in both the early stages of the survey program and the late stages. Five specific threats, and their potential remedies, are considered here:

1. Senior management does not see the value proposition.
2. Survey findings are not linked to business issues.
3. The organization lacks a strong follow-up process.
4. Management does not have the skills needed for effective follow-up.
5. Accountability for improvement is lacking.

Senior Management Does Not See the Value Proposition

Senior management may not see the potential value of a survey program if it is not apparent that the survey is linked to business outcomes. This may happen for the following reasons:

- The survey is not tailored to the organization's unique strategy and business objectives.
- Senior management sees that the survey is entitlement focused, grounded in employee satisfaction alone rather than in strategic people issues.
- The survey is viewed as just another HR program, not an effort closely linked to business goals.

These concerns can be avoided with a strategic approach to survey design and development, as described in Chapter 5. Organizations should involve senior management from the outset of the program, ask them the three questions that link business strategy to people issues, and develop items that reflect the organization's strategy and business conditions.

A senior HR executive in a utility noted:

> "The most important part is the upfront work and achieving complete clarity on what the organization most badly wants to know that it is worth fixing. Commitments to act on the results should be made up front, and the survey providers should make this discussion as concrete as possible, such as, 'Some organizations like yours get results that suggest . . . What might your company do to respond to findings like this?' Surveys to merely satisfy curiosity about what employees are thinking or feeling are likely to fail."

Survey Findings Are Not Linked to Business Issues

Even if the survey is well designed, it must be analyzed in a way that links the results to business issues and that identifies high-priority issues for action. The problem of not linking survey findings to business issues can be avoided by using the following:

- Data reports that provide a concise overview of strengths and concerns for the organization as a whole and for various business units, departments, and geographies
- Driver and linkage analyses that pinpoint the highest-priority issues for action, both organization-wide and for units, departments, and locations

The Organization Lacks a Strong Follow-Up Process

As noted earlier in this chapter, the failure of survey programs is often a result of flaws in the follow-up process. Typical flaws at this phase include the following:

1. Failure to provide rapid feedback
2. Lack of a clear follow-up road map to address the chief issues; this map is closely linked to identification of high-priority issues for action, as noted above, but also includes development, communication, and implementation of a plan for rolling out the results and conducting action planning sessions
3. Lack of clear action plans, goals, measures, and milestones
4. Absence of a structured reporting and monitoring system for capturing action plans, tracking progress toward goals, and sharing solutions across the organization

These issues can be avoided with development of a comprehensive, top-down action planning process as described previously in this chapter. The process must be designed to focus attention on the critical organization-wide and local issues, must be well communicated, and must include a good monitoring and reporting system.

Management Does Not Have the Skills Needed for Effective Follow-Up

Strong managers will be able to run with results, but many managers will need training, coaching, and support, even with a good follow-up process. Earlier in this chapter we recommended comprehensive training programs to address this concern.

Accountability for Improvement is Lacking

Action plans not accompanied by specific goals, measures, and accountabilities are at risk for failure. Accountabilities must be built into the action planning process, beginning at the top of the organization. As Darren Smith, a measurement specialist for a federal agency recommended asking, "Do managers who are expected to make change leap at the opportunity to be accountable for such changes? If not, why not?" Specific timetables, milestone measures, and tracking tools like pulse surveys can be used to support accountability throughout the organization.

Action Tips

1. Make the survey follow-up process in your organization highly visible. Begin with communicating the overall results in writing or in town-hall forums, and move quickly to action planning sessions on a few key issues. Keep communications alive as issues are surfaced, solutions are developed, and solutions are implemented. Ongoing active communications keep the survey and the follow-up process alive over time and help ensure receptivity to surveys conducted later.

2. Wherever possible, have managers run the action planning sessions in their own units. If survey results indicate that the managers will have problems conducting the sessions, provide them with coaching and training and co-lead the sessions with them as required.

3. Put a visible measurement and tracking system in place. Comprehensive follow-up software packages that are readily available enable managers to post their action plans and to report on milestones and allow those overseeing survey follow-up to monitor the process.

4. Hold managers accountable for follow-up. Managers should commit to action on a selected few issues, and their performance should be tracked. This step should occur at all levels at which action plans are expected, starting with the leadership team of the organization.

IV

USING SURVEY INTELLIGENCE TO MAKE KEY TALENT DECISIONS

As we stated at the beginning of this book, survey and other diagnostic information is underutilized in organizations as a tool for providing strategic and tactical information for making decisions. In Section III, we focused on the decision-making and talent-optimizing opportunities that more omnibus employee surveys afford. Though these surveys offer an excellent opportunity to capture helpful information for decision making, survey tools and related assessments have numerous other applications that go underutilized in far too many organizations.

The prior section focused mostly on optimizing your existing workforce. But what information can we obtain that will help us hire more effective talent? And how can surveys or other diagnostics help us retain good performers or recover them in the future? How can we use survey information to optimize our leaders and their performance?

In this section, we will address a number of decisions being made every day in organizations that can be aided by better information. Historically, obtaining this information was cost prohibitive for many organizations, but with the advent of new technology and more advanced organizational effectiveness models such as People Equity, gaining competitive advantage in new ways is now possible—by leveraging talent more capably, by generating greater innovation, by eliminating huge waste, and by taking advantage of new opportunities currently missed. If you do not utilize this information and your competitors do, they will have the wind at their back in your race for success.

Chapter 8 will focus on the early stages of the talent lifecycle (see Figure IV.1) and on employer branding, talent acquisition, and onboarding.

We will then turn to the other end of the lifecycle—retaining and recovering talent—in the Chapter 9.

In the final chapter in this section, we will focus on how information can help organizations develop leaders who optimize talent—aligning it with organizational goals, developing sufficient competencies to meet customer requirements, and creating highly engaged people whose performance is maximized.

Figure IV.1 Stages of the Talent Lifecycle

Chapter 8

Leveraging Information to Optimize Employer Brand, Hiring, and Onboarding

"I'm looking for commitment. Why do you want to be a part of our company? Why do you want to leave the company you're at now? I'm concerned about what I can't see on your resume."[1]

—F. Mark Gumz, CEO, Olympus Corporation of the Americas

In the previous section we covered the strategic use of employee surveys to optimize existing talent in organizations. Let's take a look at the organizational entry process and how surveys and similar diagnostic information can assist in decision making.

Most people using employee survey information today do not think about it in the context of hiring, and yet many connections can be made, enabling organizations to improve their talent acquisition effectiveness. What if you had information that could dramatically increase your hiring effectiveness?

Consider Some Fast Facts

The effectiveness of the hiring process in organizations bears close scrutiny:

- Hiring effectiveness in many organizations is below 50 percent—that is, less than 50 percent of hires succeed; research psychologists tell us that the average success rate hovers near 60 percent.

- One in 20 new hires quits on the first day.
- For many employers, hiring is a costly budget item, especially in higher-turnover industries or jobs or for highly paid and sought-after roles.
- As market demand has increased in a variety of job groups and regions (for example, engineers and scientists; many medical jobs; leadership roles, especially in developing countries), the cost of making poor hiring decisions is rising dramatically.
- Experts tell us that the hiring process in a majority of organizations is inefficient, leading to waste and lost candidates.
- The indirect costs of ineffective hiring can be high, in terms of lower morale of peers, frustrated customers, and ramp-up training and productivity time.

How can surveys or other information sources help? To answer that question, we will discuss two types of information: information that already exists somewhere in your organization and, second, information that could be gathered without great expense or effort. The latter is information that could be added that would provide insight into how talent acquisition could be enhanced. We will discuss both sources as we examine different stages of the talent lifecycle.

To apply the value of information, let's take a look at different parts of the talent acquisition process.

Having an Attractive Employer Brand

All organizations are concerned about attracting the right talent—talent who will be aligned with the organization's vision and mission, have the right competencies, and be engaged in their roles and in the organization's goals and culture. To attract more of the "right" talent, smart organizations are building strong employer brands or talent value propositions (some call them employer value propositions or EVPs). The talent value proposition (TVP) provides a working description of the expected exchange between an employee and employer.

That is, what does the employee expect from the organization (for example, compensation and benefits, autonomous working environment, creative people), and what, in turn, does the employer expect from the employee (for example, long work hours, creative output, and adherence to its values)? A TVP usually consists of five to seven core distinguishing attributes of your organization and sometimes supporting elements. These distinguishing attributes are intended to answer the question: Why do you deserve to attract and retain great talent? Abridged sample TVPs are provided in Table 8.1.

In building a TVP, it is essential to define the attributes well, understand where you stand today, and map out the challenges that must be overcome and resources needed to arrive at the desired state. An example work plan for one attribute, adaptability, is listed in Table 8.2.

A TVP is not about trolling for any available talent; it is about casting a targeted net to find those in the marketplace who have the potential to be a good fit. If you are not as good as your competitors in this space, they will have better talent to choose from.

As depicted in Figure 8.1, an organization not only must create an attractive brand, but those brand attributes exemplified in the TVP will be tested by candidates both during the hiring process and on the job. It is imperative that the brand be conveyed consistently and lived, or the organization will lose credibility either during the hiring process or shortly after new hires arrive.

Table 8.1 Samples of Abridged Talent Value Propositions

Ritz Carlton

The Employee Promise: At The Ritz-Carlton, our Ladies and Gentlemen are the most important resource in our service commitment to our guests. By applying the principles of trust, honesty, respect, integrity and commitment, we nurture and maximize talent to the benefit of each individual and the company. The Ritz-Carlton fosters a work environment where diversity is valued, quality of life is enhanced, individual aspirations are fulfilled, and The Ritz-Carlton Mystique is strengthened.

Marriott

Where life just keeps getting better.

You've found a place where you define what success means to you, and we help make it happen. It's where you'll be given the building blocks you need to forge a challenging new path, the hotel jobs/ opportunities you want to expand your skills, and the benefits that let you live the life you want.

Table 8.2 A Sample Work Plan for Adaptability as Part of a Talent Value Proposition

Employer Target Attribute	Adaptable
Operational Definition	The willingness and ability to respond rapidly to a variety of employee and customer needs
Current Now	Responsive to customers or the CEO in a reactive fashion, but no proactive plan, capabilities, or approach has been developed
Could Be	People anticipate and meet changing customer and employee expectations in a systematic way
Rationale	Employees who feel ownership for the business will likely contribute more time and energy to meet customer needs
Barriers to Change	Conflicting priorities, high demands on limited resources, lack of engagement, lack of trust in management
Resources Required	Clear goals and priorities, senior role modeling, and respect for others

How Can Surveys Help?

Information related to the TVP can easily be obtained from ongoing surveys of your existing workforce and other observers of your culture, such as suppliers. For example, if "innovative" and "entrepreneurial" are core differentiators of your organization, current employees ought to endorse those qualities. These elements can be built into your existing employee survey as a TVP index. If you are not currently living the TVP or it is aspirational, survey data from existing employees will provide valuable information on the gaps and where to put future emphasis to close the gaps. An example of a five-item index is shown in Table 8.3.

Another valuable perspective is that of recent hires. Surveys of those who have recently arrived, or segmentation of the workforce by those with short tenure in surveys administered to the larger

Figure 8.1 Brand Alignment

Table 8.3 Sample TVP Index

TVP challenge items for the firm branding itself as entrepreneurial, innovative, flexible, environmentally conscious, and respected in the market.
1. XYZ is an entrepreneurial workplace in which employees have a great deal of latitude to operate.
2. XYZ is an innovative organization in which employees are expected to be creative in constantly innovating products and processes.
3. XYZ is a flexible work environment in which there are few rules and employees are given the freedom and responsibility to accomplish their work assignments in ways that balance their personal and team needs.
4. XYZ is an environmentally conscious organization that cares about the environment and encourages employees to conserve natural resources and behave in responsible ways.
5. XYZ is respected in our industry and the communities in which it operates.

workforce, can provide current information on the employer brand in the marketplace, brand communications during the hiring process, and the reality of what they have seen since they arrived.

Talent Acquisition Process Effectiveness

Recent hires can provide something additional. They have just been through the hiring process and will be able to report on its effectiveness through the eyes of an applicant. They can report on its efficiency and on whether it made them more or less enthusiastic about the organization (for example, "I still came despite the process, which really turned me off").

Sites like Glassdoor provide rapid real-time feedback on how the organization is perceived by those who have interacted with it; for larger organizations, these sites are likely to offer a variety of comments—positive and negative—about their processes (see sidebar for two examples from Walmart). Applicants who do not receive job offers do not submit exclusively negative comments; if processes are well designed and communicated, many who are turned down will have positive things to say about the organization and the process. Also, organizations often see variance on such sites because potential candidates have interacted with different parts of the organization, often finding different experiences depending on whom they met and how the process was handled.

Below are two examples of comments from those who have interacted with Walmart in the recruiting process:

Negative: "Behavior based interview. Culture is risk averse, insular. The company evades questions about benefits, work environment, business hours, training and orientation. Make sure you know what you are getting into."

Positive: "It was very efficient from the initial phone interview to on site to getting an offer, all within 2 weeks. I met with probably around 5 people and since it was a graphic designer position, I had to present my portfolio but it was a piece of cake really. They were mainly interested in your skill sets and your background working with marketing since that role was mainly supporting marketing."

Additionally new hires can provide insights into the communications packaging, recruiting process, selection steps, and preparatory information that occurred before they arrived. These insights can be gleaned by conducting a separate targeted survey or interview. At the same time, these tools can also address issues of onboarding and acculturation, which will be discussed shortly.

Finally, a TVP cannot be effective if it is not aligned with the passions of your CEO and the questions that he or she is likely to ask when hiring. Take Chris Barbin, CEO of Appirio, an information technology company, who says his company hires for three dominant factors: trust, professionalism, and gray matter.[2] If the TVP, company and job descriptions, and the hiring processes are not aligned with these factors, there will be much confusion, frustration, and poor-fit hires.

What If They Don't Come?

Two other candidate groups are of importance for hiring: those who never applied but who would make great employees and those who turn down offers. We will take a look at both.

Candidates who turn down offers present a unique situation. The organization believed that these individuals were qualified and a good fit, but something precluded them from accepting offers. Information about this group is particularly valued in highly competitive fields. For example, organizations such as Qualcomm have conducted surveys of those who have not accepted a job offer from the company. The surveys are designed to uncover the specific reasons for declined offers and provide critical insights into the company's selection and interviewing process. The cost of making incorrect hiring decisions is high, and investing in this type of research can save a company time and money.

If they withdrew because of something occurring in the hiring process that is controllable, then the organization needs to evaluate that issue and make corrections. One medical organization that we know well always kept applicants waiting for interviews, especially those with top management. One applicant told us he waited for over two hours for one of the interviews. That really turned him off, and apparently many others as well.

Candidates who have declined an offer are also another source of information about the overall brand and the TVP. What caused them to be interested in the first place, and what turned them off or caused them to choose elsewhere? It is easy to become defensive and to assert that "they are the losers," but in reality another organization has acquired talent you considered to be a good fit and highly qualified. Table 8.4 contains some sample areas that might be queried to help make decisions about the process. The missing information could be obtained through surveys, although interviews

Table 8.4 Potential Issues to Probe with Offer Rejections

- Were you turned down for an alternative job, or did the candidate decide to stay with an existing position?
- Alternatives being considered—were they competitive to your organization?
- What key features distinguished your organization?
- What features were less attractive in your organization?
- Which featured tipped the decision?
- Do candidates' perceptions match your espoused values?
- What impact did communication and information packaging play in the no-go decision?
- Did candidates turn down the role because of accurate perceptions?
- Were the decision factors under your control?
- Would the candidates recommend others to your firm? If not, why not?

might provide more depth of understanding. If interviews are used, however, remember to score the information so you can later tell if you are improving or not.

The second group of interest is the individuals who are qualified but never apply or are not identified as candidates. These situations represent lost opportunities. What if you missed the next Steve Jobs, assuming his characteristics were the ones you were looking for? One of the key questions here is why have we not connected with these folks? They are potentially qualified and a good fit, but for some reason they have not been reached or do not see your organization as attractive. One reason may be brand reach. The organization's marketing and brand simply do not reach the desired individuals. Another is that when the brand is heard, it does not connect with the qualified candidates for some reason. Organizations committed to diversity learned long ago to take their brand to a broader array of communities and schools and to tailor their messaging appropriately to expand their candidate pool.

Surveys can be a useful learning tool and a way to lay the groundwork for improved outreach. For example, great insight can be gained by surveying the potential applicant population to get a better sense of your employer brand. What do new college graduates think about your brand? Are you on the radar? Do they have positive or negative perceptions about your organization as a place to work? Another population is employees working for competitors or in a similar industry. What do they think of your organization—both the good and the weak points? What would attract or repel them?

One CEO with whom we have worked thinks that every prospect should believe that his firm is organizational nirvana—that candidates come because of the compelling mission. Though this is an important draw—the company changes the world through its medical interventions—young, high-flying talent may not consider this organization as the employer of choice compared to others with similar interesting missions, especially if the conditions are not right. Candidates may be concerned about balancing family needs, geographic impediments, educational aspirations, and so forth.

One of the authors recently visited the new Deloitte University which is dedicated to learning and leader development. When potential prospects consider a consulting organization in the context of their own development, this visible commitment to education by Deloitte may be a distinct advantage over others with an equally interesting mission but perhaps not such a visible educational differentiator.

A survey of the population of potential applicants can provide a vast amount of competitive information about the attractiveness of the employer brand. The sampling of these populations is a nontrivial research challenge, but organizations do it every day. Strongly branded organizations or emerging firms that need to be on the radar of a particular employment group perform surveys of potential applicants. The sampling issues are beyond the scope of this book, but nevertheless if done well, the data provide targeted information about how your firm can attract a stronger share of the "right" talent.

Talent Acquisition Processes: Recruiting and Selection

We know from a good deal of research that organizations have been far more focused on testing for competencies than on selecting for fit. Fit could include alignment with the organization's mission and vision, but it could also include the likelihood that an individual will be engaged with the culture. For example, someone who is an individualist may feel overwhelmed in an enveloping team environment. Or someone who is used to diverse, multicultural environments may feel estranged in a more monocultural climate. Chris Barbin, the Appirio CEO cited earlier, noted that two of his company's co-founders are Naval Academy graduates, who demand professionalism, "Do you return a phone call right away? Do you respond to your e-mail? Do you show up on time for a meeting?"[3] Obviously, people for whom this is a turnoff will not fit this culture well.

Although organizations have improved dramatically over the past thirty years in testing for competencies and in hiring people who meet certain performance and ability standards, their effectiveness at measuring Alignment and Engagement is considerably weaker. These are often difficult to test for; instead, questionnaires, interviews, and other tools may be of help. For example, few organizations use surveys of cultural fit or style for assistance in finding good fit. Table 8.5 provides a sample of items that might help a high-tech entrepreneurial firm look for fit. Without identifying these factors that may disqualify an otherwise competent prospect, hiring is a bit like throwing dice.

Another consideration is the high cost of hiring. Karl Ahlrichs, a Consultant at Gregory & Appel Insurance, asserts that current hiring processes waste time and fail to spot high performers who will fit the company's culture.[4] Moreover, organizations do not apply knockout factors early enough in the selection process when costs are lower. Questions that may rule out fit might be asked on the website or earlier in the process (1) to discourage some prospects from applying and (2) to lead to an early discussion that may eliminate a candidate. For example, one medical organization realized that its

Table 8.5 Sample Alignment Topics That May Create Good Fit

Highly collaborative; team-based decision making	↔	Highly independent; autonomous decision making
Lots of chaos and disorder	↔	An orderly, planful environment
Clear decision rules	↔	Decisions are crafted to the situation
Customer needs drive most of our actions	↔	Innovation drives most of our actions as we create *new* customer needs
Open-communication environment	↔	Need-to-know environment
Leaders drive most decisions	↔	Leaders are coaches and support line-facing employees
Strong service orientation	↔	Strong efficiency orientation
High-risk, high-reward environment	↔	Low-risk, modest-reward environment
Strong job security	↔	Job security is based on individual and unit value
Creative	↔	Predictable
High-personal growth environment	↔	Lower personal growth but stable environment
High-support environment (for example, services)	↔	"Do it yourself" culture

CEO rejected a large number of people because of his style and feelings about fit, so for key hires, they started with the CEO rather than ended with him.

Organizations must be cautious to comply with fair employment regulations so that fit does not become a way to discriminate against protected classes of employees.

Another risk is erring too much on the side of total fit, creating a situation in which new ideas and diverse experiences are missed, greatly reducing innovation and adaptability for the organization.

By obtaining information such as that in Table 8.5, your organization may be able to build over time a database of the characteristics that are most likely to succeed in your culture. For example, entrepreneurial self-starters may have an edge in your environment over those who need more support and job security. By doing these types of data analyses, making your talent acquisition processes more effective is possible, with fewer false positives among the hires.

Onboarding

Once hired, employees must be brought into the organization in a way that not only teaches them your operating practices but also acculturates them. Surveys and other diagnostics should play a crucial role at this stage.

Figure 8.2 shows why onboarding is so important. When new employees begin with an organization, Engagement is quite high; after all, these individuals have made a major life change in coming to your organization and usually have high expectations of success and fulfillment.

Alignment, on the other hand, is usually much lower; new hires have yet to learn the ropes and are only beginning to understand the values and "the way things are really done around here," as one of our recent interviewees said. They must learn more about the goals, how to align with peer organizations, how the organization aligns with its customers, and so forth. CEO F. Mark Gumz of the Olympus Corporation of the Americas, for example, prefers to hire people who can join a collegial group: "You're not going to make it here if you're

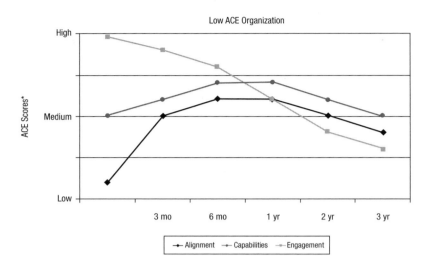

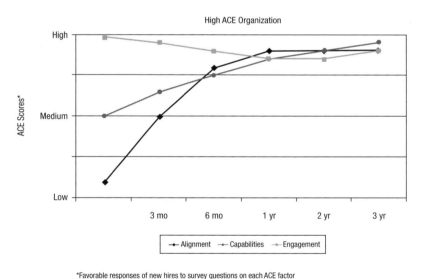

*Favorable responses of new hires to survey questions on each ACE factor

Figure 8.2 Potential Profiles of New Hires on ACE as They Acculturate

going to try and change the company immediately. You're going to have to merge into traffic. You're not going to come onto the highway at 80 miles per hour. If you do that, you're going to cause an accident."[5] He wants new hires to understand the "rules of the road"—Alignment—before they begin to adapt them.

Capabilities may start high or low, much depending on the organization's approach to hiring and also on the level of the position. Some organizations hire people who are expected to hit the ground running and who are usually selected for high-existing competencies; however, they may or may not have the information and resources needed to deliver high results to their customers yet. Other organizations hire raw talent with the idea of shaping it and developing it. In these organizations, Capabilities may initially be lower because the organization will develop the competencies (one factor in Capabilities) along the way. Management trainees, for example, are not expected to have proven Capabilities—here we would be much more concerned with Engagement and potential Alignment characteristics.

Figure 8.2 provides a comparison of the profiles of two organizations—one with high ACE and one with low. We already know the negative financial, customer, and employee outcomes of having low ACE. However, without measures in place early and along the acculturation process, we do not have much information allowing us to intervene as needed to shape higher ACE.

Smart organizations today obtain survey information early in the process. We are told by psychologists that new hires make early judgments about fit—some as early as the first day! Without data to track fit, it is hard to intervene in a problematic manager-employee situation or to identify managers having more difficulty acculturating new hires. With early survey information on Alignment, Capabilities, and Engagement and the Drivers of success—for example, initial impressions of the cultural norms, expectations about training, leader support, fairness, and communication adequacy—human resources or other leaders can take actions before good talent is lost, or before productivity fails to reach acceptable standards.

We strongly recommend discussions with new hires as well. If you hire enough employees in a given period, focus groups can unveil meaningful information about the organization and the acculturation process. For example, Novartis Oncology conducts regular breakfast meetings with leaders to see how things are progressing. What do new hires like or dislike? What would be more helpful for them and for future hires? Answers to these questions enable the company to improve its onboarding and to accelerate acculturation.

Though early assessment is good, we have found that frequent tracking for new hires is warranted. A 30-, 90-, and 180-day schedule is not unreasonable for tracking changes as new hires are acculturated. Table 8.6 provides some ideas about issues that may be worthwhile to assess.

One important note here: Ongoing tracking surveys can either be combined with broader employee surveys or be kept as a separate tool. We will discuss this in more depth in Chapter 18 as we look at integrated intelligence systems. The key is to conduct surveys early and regularly and to take actions based on the information that will not only improve the onboarding process but also help evaluate and make changes to the hiring process and communications.

Table 8.6 Useful Issues to Probe with Surveys and Interviews during the Onboarding Stage

Perceptions of the hiring process:
- Efficiency
- Attractiveness
- Communication
- Expectations

Alignment issues:
- Understand company direction?
- Understand how role supports that direction?
- Horizontal alignment: relationship with peer and partner organizations
- Customer alignment: understanding who internal or external customers are and how the new hire's role links to them
- Brand awareness and implications for internal behaviors

Capabilities issues:
- Competencies to deliver high value to customers
- Information adequacy
- Resource adequacy
- Teamwork

Engagement issues:
- Supervisory support (for example, communication, fairness)
- Recognition culture
- Training and development (against expectations)
- Communications adequacy and openness
- Job characteristics (for example, challenge, autonomy, complexity)

Expectations against promise:
- Compensation and rewards
- Supervisor
- General support (for example, child care, flexibility, technology)

In this chapter, we have looked at additional uses of employee surveys beyond broader Engagement, ACE, or workforce surveys described in Section III. In particular we have focused on their use in managing the brand, talent acquisition, and onboarding. We recommend complementing quantitative measures with qualitative ones, such as interviews or focus groups, to obtain more in-depth understanding of issues. The value of surveys or other systematic quantitative measures is that they are cost-effective and provide tracking data so we can tell how we have changed over time.

In the next chapter, we will discuss the other end of the talent lifecycle—retaining and recovering talent.

Action Tips

1. Do you have sufficient information to understand what attracts employees to your organization? Consider creating measures that help you identify how you can differentiate your organization from competitors, including creating a talent value proposition (TVP) and testing it in the market and with current employees.
    a. Are your interview questions designed to both send and receive messages connected to your TVP?
    b. Are your selection criteria aligned with the TVP?
    c. Are managers evaluated on how well they support the TVP?

    Also, does your organization understand what drives Engagement among already successful employees? Do you measure those factors in the hiring process?
2. Is your hiring process efficient? Consider surveying prospects and recent hires to determine how you can improve the value of the process and make it more efficient and effective.
3. How well do you onboard and acculturate new hires? Consider gathering information through surveys and interviews on the acculturation process beginning shortly after hire. Do your measures tell you how well your acculturation process

is aligned with your TVP? If you sell teamwork strongly in your TVP, but new hires find themselves struggling without much team support during acculturation, is it a disconnect that must be corrected?

Chapter 9

Using Information Tools to Retain and Recover Talent

"More than three-quarters of departing employees say they wouldn't recommend their employer to others."[1]
  —Corporate Executive Board, 2011

In Chapter 8, we discussed the application of survey and other diagnostic or needs assessment tools to the branding and talent acquisition processes. Figure IV.1, depicted at the beginning of Section IV, showed the overall talent lifecycle that needs to be managed. And of course, management requires good measurement. Let's now go to the end of the lifecycle to take a look at talent retention and talent recovery.

Retention of Good Talent

"This is a topic that is near and dear to our hearts," says Robert Hoffman, Vice President of Leadership and Organizational Development at Novartis Oncology. Though his company's Engagement scores were high, survey results indicated that an increasing number of employees could be retention risks. Leaders in every organization we have met say that they want to retain their best talent. Despite this assertion, we continue to be amazed at how few use measurement effectively to understand and manage talent retention. Even those who do often then fail to take appropriate interventions. The "science" of retention is quite intricate, but it does not require sophisticated tools to manage.

In the retention arena, several questions help identify retention areas of focus and guide the selection of the best diagnostic tools to understand and better manage turnover. Let's start with the strategic considerations first and then move on to the tactical ones:

1. What talent is most important to the organization? In most organizations there are "A" jobs, as Richard Beatty and his colleagues have noted, that produce more value to the organization.[2] John Boudreau and his colleagues have argued that a better question is "What talent is most pivotal?" Pivotal talent exists where improving the quantity or quality of the talent has the greatest impact on organizational success.[3] And they are not always obvious. At Disney theme parks, for example, Boudreau and Ramstad[4] demonstrated that street sweepers can be more influential to customer loyalty than the Disney characters in costume. In your organization, what are the roles that could make or break the business? Which roles might provide the most satisfaction to customers? These are the roles that we most want to protect from unnecessary turnover.

2. In what roles might it be hardest to replace talent? Are geologists or chemical engineers almost impossible to find in your industry or geography? Perhaps software talent or critical care nurses have formidable replacement challenges. If so, these roles may be on your A-list as well.

3. How much does replacing a particular employee or job type cost? Potential occupants of a role may be plentiful but difficult or expensive to recruit, compensate, and get to peak performance; senior managers come to mind, but a role like a service representative in a telecom call center could be equally challenging. Some service rep roles require over four months of training, and the failure rate is still quite high. What have you invested in high potentials who may not yet be in principal roles?

4. Who are your pivotal employees? These may be your best performers today. We all know that replacing an A performer is far more challenging and less likely to be successful than replacing the average performer. However, a number of organizations are also looking at B players these days in a new light. These people are often steady performers who may have critical knowledge of customers, processes, or other factors that make their retention highly valuable to the organization. Another type of pivotal employee identified by Karen Stephenson's research is often hidden from view.[5] These are employees who serve as information hubs or gateways for knowledge or influence. Certain employees, despite the same job title or position in the formal structure, control far more decisions and influence many more people than their counterparts. Others operate informally as gatekeepers, who because of their position in the informal and social structure can withhold information or access. All of these must be considered in thinking about pivotal employees.

5. Who are your high potentials? As noted earlier, they may be gems in the rough and may not yet be in top roles, may not have deep customer or process knowledge yet, may not be gatekeepers or in the highest-cost roles, but they may be future performance leaders for the organization. And often, organizations have invested considerably in their long-term development.

Once we have thought through these issues, how can we better understand why we lose talent in these key groups or roles, and how can we better manage and reduce loss? This is where the right data are worth their weight in gold. Data can help address three key questions. The first question is: Why is the turnover occurring when and where it occurs? For example, the organization may lose people with two to three years of service, or it may lose people from locations in which it is too expensive to live or too challenging, such as in a less-developed or high-risk country. The second question is: How can we better control turnover? Surveys and interviews can be highly informative in understanding why turnover occurs and even more beneficial in understanding if and how we can improve it. The third question is, how can we predict who we will lose, who will be successful, and who will need development to be successful?

In the Novartis Oncology example, the company's survey first told executives that they had increased risk of losing good talent. Second, it pointed them to career development as a key driver of retention. It further directed them to the groups of employees most vulnerable. These data enabled the company to establish stay interviews, which managers conducted with current employees. Using this information, the managers were more effective at matching company career support to individual needs.

What Is Causing Turnover?

The answer to this question is best understood through the eyes of employees who have departed and those who remain with the organization, as well as through some savvy organizational analyses. Both groups have compelling perspectives on the retention issue. Let's first look at those who have already departed. Clearly, they have taken the ultimate step of separation.

Dearly Departed—The Fallacy of Exit Data

Most firms collect exit data on departing employees, often in the form of interviews or exit surveys. However, much of this information is worthless. Either it is not summarized or integrated into useful information, or it is plain wrong. Employees are not always as candid as we would like when they provide information on why they are leaving. And why would they be? They might need future references. Smart people do not burn bridges. Our estimates are that 50 percent of exit data may be flawed, providing incorrect conclusions as to why people are leaving the organization. Especially vulnerable are reasons related to people—their supervisor or peers—the very people they may need in the future. Or they may not want to admit they are stressed beyond ability to cope or that they do not buy in to the new direction of the firm.

Whatever the case, we recommend a stronger practice. A brief survey administered by a third party at the time of departure is more likely to produce accurate data. However, a growing practice is to sample employees with a survey or interviews three to nine months after they have separated from the organization. In one diagnostic company, for example, the ostensible reason for sales force departures was more pay and less administrative hassle. But after many of these representatives were interviewed after six to twelve months in their new roles, most did not achieve windfall increases in pay, and their real frustrations were high, given a lack of new products to sell and sales managers who were not helping them succeed.

There are several reasons why delayed information capture is beneficial:

- In cases where the separation involved a good deal of emotion, much of this emotion will have passed, and the employee may be in a better state of mind for candid discussion. If there was animosity on the corporate side, much of this will have been abated.

- Employees will have been in new positions for a few months or more and will be able to provide some comparison of the two cultures, reflecting on where the "grass is greener" and where it is not. By waiting until they have passed the initial three-month honeymoon period, you are more likely to obtain comparative information that could be useful in understanding why they left and the relative attractiveness of the two organizations. Usually, you will find aspects of your culture or characteristics of your organization that were viewed as less attractive and others that are actually missed. The latter provide a useful strength index for building communications to potential new hires.

How should this information be gathered? Surveys to a sample or to all separated employees in the target categories described above—most strategic roles, top performers, and more—are usually most effective. Some organizations prefer to collect such information on all employees so that comparisons across such groups as minorities and generational cohorts, supervisors, or divisions can be made. A short five- to ten-minute targeted survey with fifteen or so questions can provide ample information on the dimensions in Table 9.1. However, the organization must first set expectations that it will be conducting the survey and must keep in touch with former employees. We find that third-party information collection provides the most objective information. Let's face it—even three months after an employee's departure, a call by the local HR representative or his or her former boss is unlikely to elicit much more detail than it did when the employee left. Some organizations use gift cards, contributions to a favorite charity, or other incentives to ensure sufficient participation.

Great Practice

Though we find that surveys provide good representative information, when coupled with interviews, the information can be far more powerful. The interviews, again by a neutral party, enable the interviewer to dig deeply behind questions to uncover more about the dynamics of the situation—especially when sensitive issues are involved, such as an abusive supervisor, questions of fairness, or a personal problem. Says Marisa Harris, former VP of Human Resources for CIT, "You need a third party to create trust and a promise of confidentiality."

Table 9.1 Useful Information from Post-Employment Surveys

- Primary and secondary (very important!) reasons for leaving
- Perceptions of former supervisor
- Company values
- For shorter-tenure staff, how the employer promise (or TVP, described in Chapter 8) lived up to the communications. Was the organization as truly entrepreneurial as it claimed it was? Are people really given autonomy if that was promised?
- Comparisons of key cultural values between former employee's job at your company and their new job
- Departed employees' expectations, elicited from targeted questions
- Would departed employees consider returning to the organization at some point in the future?
- Would they recommend others to the organization?

Saving Those in the Boat—Increasing Retention in Your Current Workforce

The viewpoints of current employees provide another perspective on turnover that is worth considering for two reasons. First, they can offer their opinions about why past employees have left—not only those in the past six months but over a longer period of time. Second, they can express their own perspectives on why they stay or might leave. As mentioned at the beginning of the chapter, Novartis Oncology used its survey information to address turnover risks proactively. This process led it to a better understanding of employee differences in why they like to work for the company. Using stay interviews conducted by managers, the company identified which people simply love the work they are doing, which like the money primarily, and which like the opportunities for global advancement. Says Robert Hoffman, "Once managers understand the unique motivations of their people, they can do everything possible to maximize the employee's ability to realize that need."

To obtain this information we have found that a multimethod approach works best. First, we will describe how surveys with retention indices can provide powerful information. Then we will describe how more qualitative data can fill in missing information. Finally, we will take a quick look at analytics that can be performed with the prior two sets of data or from already existing data that can be mined in your organization.

Survey with Retention Index

As Novartis Oncology did in our opening example, consider building a retention index into your existing survey or at least including a few questions that have been proven to predict turnover, such as employee intentions to remain with the organization in the next six to twelve months. Assuming the survey is conducted by a third party, the advantage is that employees can feel comfortable honestly stating their feelings about whether they expect to leave or about their unbridled loyalty or something in between.

Another advantage of the survey is that you should be able to create a solid predictor of the expected future turnover for particular groups, when market conditions permit. There is usually a ratio of intent-to-leave vs. those who actually do. Many people have periods in which they may wish for a change but in the harsh light of day realize they have a decent job and probably would not leave unless conditions were far worse. By tracking these intentions vs. actual turnover (and controlling for market conditions),[6] you can obtain a leading indicator of likely turnover in the next quarter or year, and if the levels are beyond your scorecard targets, take appropriate actions. But what actions should you take?

A well-designed strategic survey will help you determine what actions to take, and a good retention survey will include the frequent drivers of turnover. We will address this topic in the "analysis of information" section below. In working with a global financial services company, we obtained information that related the top drivers of turnover to immediate managers, growth and development, and inclusion:

- Relating to managers, items addressing *trust and effectiveness* were most important:
  - I can believe what my immediate manager says.
  - My immediate manager is effective at managing people.
- Opportunity to *achieve career objectives* was the key driver of growth and development.
- Regarding inclusion, the key drivers included *being treated with respect* and working in a unit that *encourages new ideas and different points of view.*

Knowing this information, it is possible to now evaluate the cost-benefit of trying to reduce the turnover.

Let's apply this cost-benefit thinking to an example. If pay were a cause, one would have to evaluate the return on investing more in pay compared to what would be saved in turnover costs. Keep in mind that most organizations do a poor job of calculating turnover costs.[7] Turnover costs are often double what initial estimates indicate because organizations often leave out the costs of lost productivity and time for new hires to hit targeted performance levels. In fact, productivity may be negative for a new hire when you consider that co-workers often take time from doing their own work to help the newcomer. Other affected intangibles may include continuity with customers and customer loyalty, safety risks, loss of company knowledge, team effectiveness, and indirect costs, such as salaries of talent acquisition staff and training and replacing those who immediately fail.

On the other hand, if the cause of high turnover for a particular department or group is being treated with respect, the problem is a coaching or supervisory training issue that requires little investment beyond the time to modify behaviors. Lack of recognition is another frequent cause of turnover and one that requires only small amounts of incremental action to dramatically improve the outcome.

Focus Groups

In addition to the survey, conduct focus groups with common job groups such as engineers, clerical employees, or salespeople if those are the groups of interest based on the answers to the strategic questions described at the beginning of the chapter. Whereas the survey has the advantage of a more exact prediction of turnover and its likely root cause, focus groups provide in-depth understanding of how these drivers are operating on a day-to-day basis in your organization so that you can better assess the situation and the level of control that you may have over these root causes.

Novartis Oncology used virtual focus groups of key scientific and medical talent—groups whose skill set is highly sought after and hard to find. The survey pointed to career development as a driver of retention, but the focus groups allowed deeper root-cause analysis such as learning that managers were not comfortable having career development conversations with employees. They often felt that they either were not sufficiently familiar with all the various tools available to them, or they did not know how to responds to employees' specific request around training or new job opportunities. "These issues were easily addressed with improved communications and training for managers," reports Hoffman.

Focus groups also allow you to ask more probing questions about recently departed employees in terms of the group sense of loss and root causes that may have been shared or sensed by colleagues; perhaps the departed employees did not admit or fully articulate concerns such as performance fears or group conflict with their managers. You may also discover a collective sigh of relief regarding some departed people. We have had sessions in which we learned about dysfunctional or unethical behaviors, customer and performance shortfalls, or poor teamwork. If you learn that departed employees were real "keepers" and were well liked by their colleagues, what might have been done to create a different outcome? And what special talent or knowledge did the individual have that must be replaced?

This feedback might also be useful in thinking about recovering talent, a topic discussed later in the chapter.

Analysis of Information

Once the data are collected, they must be analyzed in a way that fosters decisions to be made. For example, categorization of turnover causes by different tenure groups, demographics, job categories, divisions, or manager groups if large enough may assist in identifying whether there are patterns distinct to a particular group. In one organization we surveyed, we found that employees classifying themselves as black were leaving at higher rates than whites, whereas Hispanics had the smallest percentage of turnover. In another firm, we found high attrition among new hires. This information will help identify both root causes and actions that can be targeted to specific groups.

Another effective tool is *driver analyses* (see Table 9.2) to identify statistically the most significant drivers of turnover. Linking departed employees to ongoing employee survey data can be powerful. Though the math is complex, the research has been done, and a strategic survey provider should be able to quickly and efficiently give you the answers. The more strategic the survey being used for the workforce, such as an ACE survey, the better the answers you will have about the causes of turnover.

Table 9.2 Key Factors and Their Relative Weight as Drivers of Turnover

Job Group A: Service employees in a retail environment	
Respect and Dignity	20%
Advancement	10%
Training	8%
Job Group B: Service employees in a call center	
Training effectiveness	30%
Open and transparent environment	25%
Workplace flexibility	18%

Recovery of Good Talent

Today, more organizations are realizing that lost talent might become gained talent in the future. McKinsey served up the "war for talent" argument in the late 1990s, and since then we have gone from talent scarcity to talent glut during the recent global recession. However, as many parts of the globe have begun recovering or are in full-growth mode, many types of talent are difficult to find or to quickly develop. Currently, there are global shortages in engineering and biotechnology skills, which require long educational cycles. Key skills in energy and medical fields are also in short supply, particularly in certain geographies. In one of the authors' (Schiemann's) recent books, *The ACE Advantage: How Smart Companies Unleash Talent for Optimal Performance*,[8] he provided a list of trends that are changing the talent equation and creating shortages in certain types of talent or in certain locations due to higher demand and lower supply (a distribution problem) of talent.

Therefore, keeping the right talent is becoming more acute. Besides, losing talent who are acclimated to your organization is costly. Replacement of good talent is far from 100 percent effective. In fact, current success rates among new hires are at best 60 percent or so; that is, only 60 percent of hires stay for a requisite period of time and reach acceptable performance levels. These statistics, of course, vary by jobs, industry, and region. Success rates in finding and keeping top talent or scarce talent are far lower. You may be faced with the fact that if you lose top talent, scarce talent, or those in pivotal jobs, you will likely have to hire perhaps two to four times as many replacements as needed to find ones that adequately replace those who left. Moreover, filling those slots will likely take much longer.

How can surveys help us in this regard? Predictive surveys, interviews, or talent discussions can help identify high-risk departments or individuals. More strategic post-exit surveys may identify individuals in these groups who may have had second thoughts about their departure—perhaps the grass did not turn out to be greener. Another probe a year or so down the road may indicate interest in returning. With a proactive approach to regrettable losses, a University of Texas health center found that it has been able to attract nearly one-fifth of departed employees back; the center contacts desirable people after they have settled into another role to see if they will consider returning.[9]

If nothing else, this approach may identify those who would recommend good candidates to your applicant pool. If someone was a top performer and thinks well of the organization, that individual could be a great source of new talent. Top performers tend to hang out with other top performers! Southwestern Energy Company developed a database of key alumni after facing stiff competition for talent in energy. Not only does the firm try to recruit former employees to come back six to nine months after they have left, but it also uses the network to recruit new talent.[10]

Leveraging alumni networks is an approach that organizations such as IBM, Deloitte, Accenture, and Microsoft have taken for a variety of reasons. If your organization is generally well regarded, having an alumni group can facilitate conversations, update alumni on new developments in your organization, and tap them for help and support. It has worked for colleges and universities for years, so why not for your organization?

But creating an alumni network cannot be done passively. You must actively manage this process so that you are building a positive group that works to your advantage rather than one that devolves into a gripe network. Accenture CEO Pierre Nanterme said, "We are also very committed to fostering and maintaining great relationships with our more than 150,000 Accenture alumni around the world."[11]

Or as Deloitte CEO Joe Echevarria commented, "Being a leader begins and ends with our people, and that includes each and every one of the truly engaged members of our alumni network. As alumni who keep connected, whose veins still run green and blue with a passion for Deloitte, your engagement helps us do what we do."[12]

Networking and focus groups—many are done electronically and remotely these days—with alumni can provide support in finding suitable job candidates, messaging to the marketplace, solving problems, and obtaining volunteers for some projects. They might also rekindle an interest in some of those alumni to return, whether in a full-time role or perhaps one of the many alternative job roles emerging today. Susan Bershad, former Johnson & Johnson Vice President, remarked, "In my experience, the more senior the alum, or the more professional the role, the more critical it is for there to be personal contact."

One caution: Some organizations have yet to come to grips with the reality of a semipermeable organization in which people come and go over time. Members of Generation X and Millennials expect to work many more jobs with many more organizations than their Baby Boomer predecessors. Some organizations still operate with a good deal of rigidity in this regard, with some executives telling us in our Executive Talent Forums that "once they leave, they are dead to us." Therefore, before you embark on a recovery strategy, you must have a culture that will appreciate such change and embrace returning employees—especially if they were your stronger players in leading roles. Cautions Bershad, "Be sure there is agreement that these are good performers and then keep a list of agreed upon regrettable loses. If senior, assign other senior leaders responsibility for keeping in touch. This works!"

This chapter has addressed the issues of measurement related to employee retention and recovery. In the next chapter we turn to a central driver of talent optimization—leaders.

Action Tips

1. Set up a process to obtain neutral, third-party information from former employees regarding their views of the

organization and the factors that they weigh in the stay-leave decision.

   a. Make sure to probe your desired employer brand and values.

   b. What factors in their new organization are more desirable, and which are less?

2. If you are conducting employee surveys in your organization, you may want to create a turnover predictor index that will give you early warnings of "hot" units, roles, and locations in which higher turnover is likely.

   a. If designed well, such indices will also tell you where to look for likely root causes.

   b. If you have such hot spots, conducting interviews or focus groups is usually valuable to understand what the deeper issues are and how they manifest themselves in the workplace.

3. Consider creating an alumni group on LinkedIn or other sites that would give you a forum for maintaining contact with regrettable losses and for staying connected for potential future recovery.

   a. Alumni groups can also be used as sounding boards for new ideas.

   b. These groups, comprising people who understood your culture and context, are often the external voice of the market.

Chapter 10

Leadership Development and Succession

"To be successful, you need great leaders who know how to optimize their talent by focusing it, developing the right capabilities and creating engagement."

—Ralph Izzo, Chairman and CEO, PSEG

What defines a leader? You are correct—a follower! Sadly, one senior HR leader told us that the general answer is "senior management." Our experience with hundreds of organizations across the globe suggests that leaders are not developed for or evaluated on the capability of creating high-impact followers or teams. Regardless of the region in which we conducted interviews, executives told us they had a shortage of the *right* leaders—leaders who can sustain performance because they are able to build high-performing teams. Whereas this finding was expected in growing markets like China or Southeast Asia, it was not expected in mature markets like Europe and the United States.

In 2007 the SHRM Foundation commissioned a study to examine the research on leader development and succession. More specifically, the aim of the study was to understand what is known about successful practices; unfortunately, the research evidence is slim at best.[1] Conflicting stories tell what the best approaches are, which competencies are most valuable, and how succession should be managed. In *The ACE Advantage*,[2] Schiemann summarized:

- Most organizations believe they do not have enough leadership bench strength.

- Leaders typically understand the "what" of performance better than the "how."
- Leaders' technical skills are often stronger than their people skills.
- Organizations may not identify the best high-potential leaders, or they may hang on to those who have been tagged high potential but are not growing into the role.

Leaders should help their teams win by achieving extraordinary results—results that outpace the competition. Three potential errors in development and succession lead to mediocre leaders:

- Overfocus on competencies that do not create results
- Overreliance on competencies rather than the behaviors that we expect those competencies to deliver
- Focus solely on business results, rather than the "how" that achieves them

The first error fails to include key people outcomes—retention, Engagement, and Alignment. The second fails to acknowledge that one may possess competencies but not execute them in practice. The third fails to understand how results are altered by people.

Our research has led us to conclude that achieving talent optimization is accomplished by doing three things right: (1) creating a team aligned with the organization's vision, mission, and values and with other units; (2) providing the right competencies, information, and resources to meet customer (or internal stakeholder) expectations; and (3) creating an engaged workforce that is willing to put in discretionary effort and to advocate on behalf of the organization. We call this approach to achieving talent optimization high People Equity, as described in Chapter 4, represented by having high Alignment, Capabilities, and Engagement, or ACE. Certain leaders will be better in certain situations. For example, a pharmaceutical leader we worked with was successful in creating a high ACE team in a start-up environment, but he began to fail miserably when the organization grew. His style and skills were attuned to creating high ACE in one situation but not in the other.

Based on our research, we believe that high People Equity or ACE is one of the best leading indicators of high results. High-ACE organizations outperform their impoverished low-ACE counterparts, so if you were running an organization, you would want your leaders to be running high-ACE units. The implications for leader development and succession are clear:

- Identify potential leaders who can develop these skills, and then help them hone their ACE leadership skills.
- Help existing managers see talent management blind spots, and close the gaps.
- Provide clear expectations for what People Leaders will need to develop and excel at, and provide developmental experiences that enable them to do so.
- Provide assessment tools to help leaders know how they compare to talent optimization best practices.

If you are going to improve, you need good feedback such as that offered by surveys and other assessments, including 360-degree reviews. In a *New York Times* interview Deborah Farrington, founder and general partner of venture capital firm StarVest Partners, remarked, "People, especially those who are goal-oriented and very high achieving, want feedback."[3] Baseline assessment tools and a plan for how to use that information can help obtain feedback. The ACE surveys discussed in Section III are one tool to use for such development. From our surveys of numerous organizations, we know that no organization has 100 percent of managers scoring high on all three factors: Alignment, Capabilities, and Engagement. If they are lucky, they may have 20 percent to 40 percent. This is both good and bad news. The good news is the fact that some percentage of the leaders are scoring "triple green"—high Alignment, Capabilities, and Engagement—proving that attaining high talent optimization within these organization settings is possible. In fact, these managers are worthy of study. What are they doing in this culture that can other managers can apply within their own organizations?

The bad news is that we need to help managers who are not triple green to improve their ability to leverage talent better to accelerate their performance and long-term results. Managers scoring at low or mid levels on Alignment, Capabilities, or Engagement can be targeted for a variety of developmental interventions. Everyone wins: The managers have enhanced their skills in key areas, which will be helpful to them throughout their careers, and the organization wins because it has strengthened its leaders.

A regional power company conducted an ACE survey. Fewer than 10 percent of "leaders" had successful ACE scores—scores greater than 80 percent favorable on A, C, and E. These scores were reflected in business results. Although the firm's safety and accident record was superb, its performance in other areas was not what it could be. The result was that a large cross section of the invested talent was not being optimized. This ACE wake-up call allowed senior executives to begin a variety of efforts to create a new class of leaders— leaders who were optimizing the talent within their control.

The company began by looking at the optimizing leaders—those with triple green scores on A, C, and E. Quite a few were located in a nuclear power facility in which the plant head supported performance results that were leveraged through aligned, capable, and engaged people. In one feedback session, in sharing some generally favorable results on their ACE scores, the plant manager pressed the group to close the ACE variance in units that were not achieving triple green. He asked his managers, "Who is responsible for optimizing our people?" And the shout came back from the auditorium of managers, "We are!" Such thinking, reinforced in this case by the plant manager, helps managers think about what they could be doing differently to achieve great results through people.

Because they saw the potential for future performance, senior executives were committed to moving the needle on their ACE scores. To that end, they committed to a strong follow-up process to take action at both the company-wide and local leader levels. For example, at the company level, executives committed to a major 360-degree feedback program to help leaders gain better insights into their strengths and opportunities for improvement. They also committed to an enhanced leader development program, with training targeted to weaker competencies and behaviors such as having critical conversations and managing conflict.

At the local level, they invested in leader training on understanding their ACE profile, identifying root causes, learning what they could personally do differently, and engaging their teams in actions that would improve A, C, or E.

As you can see from the example just cited, solutions may be supported by a variety of tools. We will take a deeper look at a few.

Leader brand is a tool suggested by a leader in an energy company. It consists of a set of agreed-on behaviors that all leaders are expected to master. As this leader stated, "It makes tangible and clear what is often intangible and unclear in organizations: how leaders are expected to behave. Discipline in this area has the potential to deliver tremendous ACE results, because too often leaders are led to believe that they have license to indulge their own personalities, however maladaptive. The result is a workforce that is confused as it is whip-sawed every time a new leader steps in."

Coaching may help many managers understand and correct their blind spots, but only if consequences for not making improvements are in place. If their units score low in Engagement, for example, a good survey will have driver items that pinpoint likely causes, such as poor recognition, ineffective communication, or weak developmental activities. This process will allow an effective coach to work with that manager to make improvements that will enhance their results.

Table 10.1 provides a list of some of the essential competencies and behaviors of supervisors and coaches in creating a high-ACE, optimized workforce.

Training is another potential intervention to enhance knowledge or build particular skills. For example, we have used ACE training to help managers better understand how they can improve one or more of the ACE dimensions. Some of the low A, C, or E scores may be due to individual manager behaviors, some to group dynamics, and still others to higher-level actions or communications. In the first two

Table 10.1 Frequent People Leader Competencies and Behaviors That Drive High Alignment, Capabilities, and Engagement

Alignment

- Strategic and critical thinking to better understand issues related to organizational direction
  ◦ Setting priorities, planning, and decision making in a strategic context
- Communicating
  ◦ Organizational direction
  ◦ Organizational, department, and individual goals
  ◦ Organizational values, such as ethics and safety
- Using performance measurement (for example, scorecards, team, and individual measures) effectively
- Connecting rewards to performance
- Facilitating interdepartmental cooperation
- Providing coaching and feedback that enables employees to improve performance and live the organizational values

Capabilities

- Matching the right talent (right competencies) with the right roles
- Providing or enabling the information needed to meet customer expectations
- Providing the right resources to meet customer expectations
- Supporting training that enables employees to meet or exceed performance expectations
- Building effective teams
- Managing conflict
- Drawing on diverse resources that will create stronger solutions, better innovation

Engagement

- Motivating different types of employees
- Treating employees fairly
- Communicating and behaving in ways that create trust and feelings of respect
- Respecting employees with diverse backgrounds
- Providing reasonable flexibility to help employees balance work and family obligations
- Recognizing employees for their contributions in meaningful and motivational ways
- Helping employees learn and grow

Source: William A. Schiemann, *Reinventing Talent Management: How to Maximize Performance in the New Marketplace* (Hoboken, NJ: John Wiley; Alexandria, VA: Society for Human Resource Management).

cases, training may be an effective tool in developing the manager's skills or the skills of the group. However, in areas where the root cause lies outside the managers' scope, training is not the answer. For example, a supervisor may communicate well, but if the company direction is poorly articulated, that manager will have difficulty scoring highly in communicating the company direction; however, there is no excuse for not having clear individual goals linked to the department's goals.

Another example might be poor teamwork. Though the manager may be espousing high teamwork, perhaps other members of the team hinder it. This type of situation may require individual intervention or perhaps team-building activities.

In any case the survey can be a great tool for sorting and prioritizing the organization's management development needs, and especially for identifying the likely gaps leading to suboptimized talent and business performance, *if the right driver items are included in the survey* (see Table 10.1 for example).

Another tool is *360-degree feedback*. This has become a popular way to provide developmental feedback to managers. We favor combining the employee survey with the other 360 perspectives (peers, manager, suppliers) because the employee survey provides a richer source of upward feedback. For example, in addition to providing feedback on the managers' behaviors and competencies, 360s also provide feedback on other aspects of a manager's domain that he or she is accountable for, such a teamwork, innovation, intergroup cooperation, and so forth.

Great Practice

To improve the effectiveness of your 360 feedback, the survey should contain questions related to ACE for each group (for example, peers, coach, supervisor) to rate:

- *Alignment.* To gain the perspective of direct reports, we usually include questions on alignment with goals and values. For peers, the emphasis might be on intergroup Alignment. For the supervisor, it might be on Alignment with the goals at that level.
- *Capabilities.* Do peers, supervisors, and employees see high teamwork within the unit, which is a Capabilities driver? Or do internal customers feel that the manager being rated has the right competencies to effectively deliver value to their units?
- *Engagement.* From an Engagement perspective, are your people seen as energized or dragging? Are you providing recognition in areas that matter to the success of the

business? Are these visible to the organization? Do others see you developing your people or your successor?

Another powerful tool connected to 360 thinking is leadership calibration sessions being used by Novartis. These sessions help calibrate talent ratings across leadership groups. Robert Hoffman, Vice President of Leadership and Organizational Development for Novartis Oncology, shared:

> We've had tremendous success with these discussions because it allows other leaders to share information/perceptions/experiences with each other about organizational talent and alleviate "blind spots" that a particular manager may have had about his/her employees. Sometimes, managers just don't have all the information about a given employee, and these calibration sessions help provide revealing information that may not have been available to the manager.

Such sessions are most effective when leadership teams agree on action plans that help provide broader exposure for an employee who is being discussed. For example, one leader might agree to meet with or even mentor an employee who works for another manager to provide greater insights into the employee's behaviors or career needs. Hoffman noted, "These actions have been a great help to our business unit in clearing up misperceptions and creating future career opportunities."

With these tools in place, coupled with strong rewards and accountabilities for development, you are likely to use your scarce resources wisely in targeted areas to optimize your leaders.

A final note on succession: We continue to find in our assessments that many leaders have been promoted across multiple levels when they are considerably short on achieving high ACE and in some cases even high business results. Many of those who have achieved positive business results did it by damaging the People Equity of the organization; they left employees in their wake who had less Engagement or whose competencies were not enhanced for future needs. Others achieved decent results to meet corporate demands, but just think what they could have achieved if their people had been highly Aligned, Capable, and Engaged.

We recommend that before promoting leaders, organizations give serious consideration to those leaders who have achieved the "what" but struggle with the "how." Survey instruments such as 360-degree feedback provide insight across multiple perspectives on precisely how the "how" is being accomplished. As one executive said, "More often than not, poor 'hows' end up hitting a wall later or destroying a lot of human capital." In any case, it costs everyone in the long run.

Action Tips

1. Consider coaching leaders on the three crucial people factors to achieve peak performance—Alignment, Capabilities, and Engagement. If leaders understand that they can achieve their goals by optimizing A, C, and E, they will be more motivated to be coached or to learn skills that will enable them to become stronger people leaders.

2. Have you used your employee survey to provide rich information feedback to managers to enable them to develop their people skills more rapidly? ACE scorecards™ and well-chosen survey items can provide useful feedback to both early stage and more seasoned managers. Often these types of survey items can be combined into leadership and supervisory indices that also predict other desirable outcomes, such as the retention of top performers.

3. Use a variety of feedback tools to help leaders understand their strengths and weaknesses in people leadership. Beyond ACE scores on their employee survey, 360-degree feedback adds perspective from peers, coaches, and customers.

4. Consider creating a "leadership brand," a set of desired leadership behaviors (not competencies). Building a leadership brand supports the talent value proposition (TVP) discussed in Chapter 8 by providing clear expectations for leader behaviors that support the TVP.

V

Managing and Measuring Values

Most organizations have a values statement. An organization's values, at times developed as a component of the overall vision and mission of the organization, indicate what is most important and provide guidelines for how work should be done.

A living value system that is top of mind for employees is a key component of Alignment, one of the critical ACE factors we have discussed throughout the book. It directs behavioral choices—the "should be" that we would like everyone in our organization to adhere to. Values can also be an enabler of Engagement. Some employees care deeply about certain values—commitment to the environment, integrity and ethical behavior, diversity and inclusion, among others. If an organization violates these values or does not support them, it can reduce commitment, one of the elements of Engagement.

Measurement is critical for bringing values to life, and an employee survey is one of the best tools for values measurement. Including a section on key values in an employee survey conveys the significance of values to survey participants and can provide feedback on both awareness of values and the extent to which the organization lives its values.

In this section we explore values, their role in the organization, and approaches to values measurement.

In Chapter 11 we consider values statements themselves, ways to embed them in the organization, the optimal number of values, and the effective use of measurement to reinforce values and track implementation. We also share examples of how fundamental values such as safety and health can drive a culture and performance.

Then, in Chapters 12 through 14, we examine three values critical to most organizations: ethics, diversity, and innovation. Ethics has been a front-burner issue for organizations for some time; it is one of the value issues most consequential for conducting business in the 21st century. The meaning of diversity and inclusion as values has evolved considerably in the past decade; ethnicity and gender issues remain relevant, but now diversity goes well beyond demographics to cover a wide spectrum of differences between individuals and groups. Innovation, a leading element of building and sustaining competitive advantage in today's global business environment, goes beyond R&D to encompass many aspects of process improvement, supply chain management, and employee involvement.

In this section we examine approaches to defining values in the context of strategy; explore ways that successful organizations address values-related challenges; and provide approaches, sample items, and survey modules for measuring organizational values.

Chapter 11

Measuring and Living Organizational Values

"Values are not just a part of the strategy—they drive the strategy and success."

—Ann Rhoades, President of People Ink and one of five founding executives and board member of JetBlue Airways

Nearly every sizable organization today espouses a set of values. Oftentimes, the values began with a founder such as Sam Walton at Walmart who built his enterprise on three core leadership values, which became known as "The Walmart Way": respect for the individual, strive for excellence, and serve your customers.[1] Robert Wood "General" Johnson built his organization on the bedrock of his famous Johnson & Johnson credo (see Figure 11.1).

In other firms, such values are developed along the way, such as those of Google, WD-40 Company, and the Ritz-Carlton. Google cofounders Larry Page and Sergey Brin say on the Google website, "We first wrote these '10 things' when Google was just a few years old. From time to time we revisit this list to see if it still holds true. We hope it does—and you can hold us to that."[2] For an excerpted summary, see the sidebar below.

Values are sometimes developed as part of the overall vision and mission of the organization. They tell us *what* is important and *how* we do things around here. Some organizations such as Qualcomm put a premium on innovation, whereas others such as Nordstrom emphasize service. CIT's Commercial Services unit developed a values state-

We believe our first responsibility is to the doctors, nurses and patients, to mothers and fathers and all others who use our products and services. In meeting their needs everything we do must be of high quality. We must constantly strive to reduce our costs in order to maintain reasonable prices. Customers' orders must be serviced promptly and accurately. Our suppliers and distributors must have an opportunity to make a fair profit.

We are responsible to our employees, the men and women who work with us throughout the world. Everyone must be considered as an individual. We must respect their dignity and recognize their merit. They must have a sense of security in their jobs. Compensation must be fair and adequate, and working conditions clean, orderly and safe. We must be mindful of ways to help our employees fulfill their family responsibilities. Employees must feel free to make suggestions and complaints. There must be equal opportunity for employment, development and advancement for those qualified. We must provide competent management, and their actions must be just and ethical.

We are responsible to the communities in which we live and work and to the world community as well. We must be good citizens—support good works and charities and bear our fair share of taxes. We must encourage civic improvements and better health and education. We must maintain in good order the property we are privileged to use, protecting the environment and natural resources.

Our final responsibility is to our stockholders. Business must make a sound profit. We must experiment with new ideas. Research must be carried on, innovative programs developed and mistakes paid for. New equipment must be purchased, new facilities provided and new products launched. Reserves must be created to provide for adverse times. When we operate according to these principles, the stockholders should realize a fair return.

Figure 11.1 Johnson & Johnson Credo
Source: Johnson & Johnson, "Our Credo," http://www.jnj.com/connect/pdf/company-pdf/our-credo.pdf

ment as part of establishing a balanced scorecard, an approach that facilitated operationalizing the values.

Ethics is one of the most significant values discussed in recent years. Concern about ethics in the 21st century kicked off with Enron, was reexamined after the Bernie Madoff scandal, and was resurfaced on a global scale with the Walmart Mexico scandal that the *New York Times* broke in 2012.[3] Because of the scale of this one value, we have devoted a separate chapter, Chapter 12, to ethics and codes of conduct.

Whatever an organization's values, measurement is a key component of bringing the values to life. Every organization has values, and every organization lives what it really values. The question is how honest an organization is about what it really values. The employee survey is an excellent tool for measuring both awareness of values and the extent to which the organization lives its values.

NOTABLE VALUES STATEMENTS

Ritz-Carlton Motto and Values (Abstracted)[4]

At The Ritz-Carlton Hotel Company, L.L.C., "We are Ladies and Gentlemen serving Ladies and Gentlemen." This motto exemplifies the anticipatory service provided by all staff members with sample service values such as:

- I am empowered to create unique, memorable and personal experiences for our guests.
- I understand my role in achieving the Key Success Factors, embracing Community Footprints and creating The Ritz-Carlton Mystique.
- I continuously seek opportunities to innovate and improve The Ritz-Carlton experience.
- I create a work environment of teamwork and lateral service so that the needs of our guests and each other are met.
- I have the opportunity to continuously learn and grow.

WD-40 Company Values[5]

- We value doing the right thing.
- We value creating positive lasting memories in all of our relationships.
- We value making it better than it is today.
- We value succeeding as a Tribe while excelling as individuals.
- We value owning it and passionately acting on it.
- We value sustaining the WD-40 economy.

Google's Philosophy and Core Principles (Abstracted)[6]

- Focus on the user and all else will follow.
- It's best to do one thing really, really well.
- Fast is better than slow.
- You don't need to be at your desk to need an answer.
- You can make money without doing evil.
- The need for information crosses all borders.

Over the years we have learned a great deal about values and how they shape organizational performance. Clear values help employees and managers choose one behavior over another when they have a choice or when they are not sure which path should be chosen. For example, "Do I pull the cord that stops the assembly line when a safety issue arises—and incur the cost of lost production?" At organizations such as DuPont, a value such as safety is sacrosanct, celebrated, and *measured.*

At BP in 2005, a few months before an explosion in the Texas City refinery, employees identified many significant safety concerns in a survey, but the information was dismissed by management as just workers' "opinions."

One of the key findings in the federal government's investigation of the 2005 Texas City refinery explosion was that "numerous surveys, studies, and audits identified deep-seated safety problems at Texas City, but the response of BP managers at all levels was typically 'too little, too late'."[7]

At the Union Carbide plant in Bhopal, India, similar patterns existed. Thousands of people were killed and maimed after a major explosion in the 1980s. In an attempt to cut expenses, only six of the original 12 operators were still working in the operation, and the number of supervisory personnel was cut in half. "No maintenance supervisor was placed on the night shift and instrument readings were taken every two hours, rather than the previous and required one-hour readings. Workers made complaints about the cuts through their union but were ignored. One employee was fired after going on a 15-day hunger strike. Seventy percent of the plant's employees were fined before the disaster for refusing to deviate from the proper safety regulations under pressure from management."[8] Clearly, there had been warning signs, but the evidence was ignored. What measures were they using—only expenses? The resulting disaster not only cost hundreds of millions but destroyed an icon in the industry.

Before it was in vogue to place such emphasis on safety, two of the authors (Morgan and Schiemann) worked with DuPont to build surveys that could assess how well the company was living the value of safety. Organizations like DuPont have a fundamental belief that *safety attitudes* affect *safety behaviors*, which in turn affect *safety results* such as injuries and lost time accidents (see Figure 11.2).

Figure 11.2 Relationship Among Safety Attitudes, Behaviors, and Results

DuPont invested heavily in safety attitude and behavior training, which had payoffs in avoiding work stoppages, injuries, or catastrophes such as the Bhopal incident that killed thousands and severely damaged Union Carbide's reputation. DuPont wanted employees to think, breathe, and live safety on the job and at home. We recall one of the leaders at its Victoria, Texas, plant talking about safety on weekends. Employees were taught how to mow their lawns safely, for example, to avoid having an employee injure him or herself. Such safety tips provide benefits to both the employee and the plant—no lost time of a valuable resource on Monday.

Because safety was a crucial value for the organization, it was included in the plant and corporate scorecards—something to be monitored and managed when scores slipped out of targeted range. DuPont's website states, "The establishment of a fully integrated safety culture leads to responsible business stewardship that motivates employees, improves performance and productivity, cuts cost and positively impacts results. We at DuPont believe that all accidents are preventable—our goal is zero injuries and zero incidents."[9]

To manage this philosophy and significant investments that supported it, we developed safety surveys that could be administered plant-wide, identifying attitudes and behaviors that were likely to influence safety. For example, if pressures for profits were to cause a plant to cut back on safety training, it would show up in the survey. The surveys also enabled management to identify risky behaviors or procedures that might compromise their safety goals before an incident occurred.

By surveying plants and comparing them, it is possible to focus on top-scoring plants as sources of best practices, as well as to identify high-risk locations that require immediate action. For those higher-risk locations, conducting more detailed assessments (for example, more detailed surveys, focus groups, and safety audits) is then good practice to identify key issues that can be corrected.

Eschew Lamination

A majority of organizations have values statements, and many have gone the route of giving every employee a list of those values laminated in plastic. Often, the values are also posted on the walls of conference rooms, in hallways, or on the organization's website. And yet, in a many of these situations we find that most employees—even senior leaders—have to look up at the wall to answer questions about their values during interviews or other discussions. Some fumble looking for their card!

Many of you know exactly what we are talking about. In these environments, values are a card—not a living commitment. This destroys the credibility of the values among both seasoned employees and new hires. People roll their eyes when we conduct focus groups asking about values in these organizations. The message is clear—"We have values in name only"—or worse, they know what is really valued, and it is not on a card. Sadly, this sentiment is more destructive than not having espoused values because it creates cynicism and mistrust. Worse yet, we never fail to find plentiful and colorful examples from focus groups, interviews, or survey write-in comments that point to senior leader behaviors that violate the values.

In our interviews with managers, we often find that they forget that values are a major driver of Alignment in an organization. When the values are living, vibrant, behavioral mantras for all employees, they focus everyone on "how" work *should* get done. Observing how it actually gets done can tell you a lot about the organization's values. A strong teamwork culture such as the one embedded in WD-40 does not tolerate poor teamwork. And it is not a management oversight role. Instead, teams—the very people who developed the company's values—enforce them and correct their fellow associates when their behaviors are out of line. These actions acculturate new employees quickly into the do's, don'ts, and *musts*.

Values are not something you have in addition to a strategy. Values are integral to the strategy. The strategy focuses people on goals, and the values focus the way we work together—that is, *how* we achieve the *goals*. Are we team or individual driven? Do we have a totally transparent communications environment, or are we more of a "need to know" firm? Do we value ethics or diversity? Is green a major part of our value system? For values to work well, an organization must identify a manageable and memorable (we do not have to read the wall plaque) set of values.

When we are working with clients on the creation or measurement of value, we are often asked how many values their organizations should have. Our first response is, What are you passionate about? What makes you want to come to work here? What makes your culture unique? If you have to measure fifteen different values, then your culture does not sound unique. Three to seven are fairly common, as that number will cover a lot of ground, yet are few enough to be remembered. Organizations can certainly have a core one, two, or three values that are powerful enough to underlie all actions and decisions. As in the earlier DuPont example, if safety was buried in a laundry list of values, how well would it have stood out or have been practiced intensively? Chris Barbin, chief executive of Appirio, says his company has three values that his executives use when hiring— trust, professionalism, and gray matter—and three values that are used to run the business—customer focus, teamwork, and fun. In an interview he said, "If you're not having fun 8 out of 10 days on a consistent basis, you've got to say something."[10]

Also, if the values are going to be lived, an investment of time and resources will be required to communicate, model, measure, and manage them. CEO Lars Bjork of QlikTech software company commented, "We developed five core values that we live by. These include challenge, move fast, be open and straight-forward, teamwork for results, and take responsibility."[11] At its annual summit, the company gives awards for each of these five categories based on employee nominations. Such recognition is striking because executives may not see how well the values are being lived.

Values provide a great example of the need for trade-offs. It is simple reality that we cannot manage a large number of priorities at the same time. We must choose. And most of us in organizations are well served to select a number of values that we are passionate about and are willing to commit time and resources to live. Only then will the measurement of them be valuable.

In the chapters that follow we will examine three special cases of values: ethics, diversity, and innovation.

Action Tips

1. Which values are most important to your organization's culture and strategic goals? Bring together a group of people from a cross section of your organization to discuss which values are most meaningful and which are being lived daily.

2. Do you have strong measurement tools to assess how well you are living the values? Employee surveys are one of the best tools for both communicating and assessing values.

3. If you use surveys, do you clearly repeat the values in the survey to remind employees what they are? This practice reinforces the values, but it should be done *after* awareness has been assessed to gain a true reading.

Chapter 12

Ethics

"Relativity applies to physics, not ethics."
—Albert Einstein

A 2012 survey of senior executives at U.S. and U.K. financial firms reported the following:[1]

- Twenty-four percent considered unethical or illegal conduct necessary for success in finance.
- Twenty-six percent said they had seen or had firsthand knowledge of wrongdoing.
- Sixteen percent would commit a crime—insider trading—if they could get away with it.

Most companies believe that they operate ethically, that their employees know what is expected of them, and that employees will "do the right thing." Says Ethics Manager Howard Winkler of the Southern Company:

> "Just this year we have added three items on our survey that
> focus on ethical culture. . . . They are intended to provide guid-
> ance in three areas: first, providing an early warning system
> for cultural breakdowns that could lead to serious misconduct;
> second, identifying issues to help shape our ethics messag-
> ing and training; and finally, giving hard data on management

> trust levels that we can share with company leadership in the
> interest of improving their ethical performance."

Yet year after year, many companies are proven wrong in ways that cost them time, money, and reputation.

In the United States before the debacle of Enron, Tyco, and others, we found few leaders interested in including ethics questions on their employee surveys. Even fewer firms were committed to special surveys or audits of ethical behaviors. But then one house of cards fell after another, resulting in congressional action and the creation of Sarbanes-Oxley and a host of other directives. Similar swings in ethics interest and legislation have been part of the long history of commerce around the world.

Best practices in maintaining the high standards dictated by numerous governing and audit bodies[2] and various European bodies[3] emphasize the need to be alert to employees' perceptions in the implementation and enforcement of an organization's code of ethics and its internal controls. Boards are now being held accountable, often through their audit committees, to evaluate *how effectively* management communicates information about the code and motivates employees to comply with the code. Under the Foreign Corrupt Practices Act (FCPA) the U.S. government can levy huge penalties against corporations for bribery or other corrupt activity outside the United States. Despite these changes, even the largest and most reputable companies can stumble.

In 2012, the *New York Times* reported a lengthy and detailed description of alleged bribery by Walmart de Mexico[4] and a cover-up— or at least turning a blind eye—by the home office in Bentonville, Arkansas. Experts were quoted estimating the cost to the company, if the allegations proved true, to be $1 billion or more under the FCPA.

Walmart provides a lengthy statement of ethics to employees, complete with examples, Q&A, help lines, and contact information. It includes guiding principles (see Figure 12.1) that emphasize integrity, following the law, and complete, truthful reporting. The guidelines

These principles are meant to help our associates make the right decisions, and to act with integrity.

- Always act with integrity.
- Lead with integrity, and expect others to work with integrity.
- Follow the law at all times.
- Be honest and fair.
- Reveal and report all information truthfully, without manipulation or misrepresentation.
- Work, actions, and relationships outside of your position with the company should be free of any conflicts of interest (discussed later in this guide).
- Respect and encourage diversity, and never discriminate against anyone.
- Ask your manager or the Global Ethics Office for help if you have questions about this Statement of Ethics, or if you face an ethical problem.
- Promptly report suspected violations of the Statement of Ethics.
- Cooperate with and maintain the private nature of any investigation of a possible ethics violation.
- When involved in an ethics investigation, you should reveal and report all information truthfully. You should present all the facts you are aware of without personal opinion, bias, or judgment.

Figure 12.1 Walmart Guiding Principles
Source: Wal-Mart, "Guiding Principles," http://ethics.walmartstores.com/StatementOf Ethics/BasicBeliefs.aspx.

are meant to help their employees make the right decisions and to act ethically. Yet, with all this in place, serious misconduct may have occurred. But even if it did not, the reputational damage is done. The measurement question is how the company could identify smoldering risks before the ethical fire. It is unclear from any public information whether in fact Walmart knew of any such risks. The lesson here is that you may have all the ethics infrastructure in place, but it is still a risk to assume you have done enough. Walmart's case and others make the point that an organization still needs an early warning system to alert it of potential problems before real damage is done.

In the last decade, corporations have been more interested in asking employee perspectives on ethical issues. Over the years, the Metrus Group has maintained a data bank of ethics questions that provides benchmarks for organizations focusing on that area (see sidebar below). We have found that ethics surveys and indices can provide early warning signals before an ethics issue blows up—

before a whistle-blowing incident. Such a survey is a safety valve for employees to signal to management that they have some concerns in the ethical arena. One organization we have worked with in this space is Kimberly-Clark Corporation.

Kimberly-Clark is a global manufacturer with a strong commitment to a worldwide Code of Conduct (CoC). The CoC is available in nearly 30 languages; all employees are trained in it, and multiple channels are available to employees for asking questions, stating concerns, or reporting issues. Each year, the company surveys tens of thousands of employees, from mill workers to the board of directors, regarding the CoC. The survey helps the company understand what employees are experiencing on the front line. If employees have observed an incident, how did they report it? What happened afterward? If they did not report it, why not? Responsibility for the survey is assigned to Internal Audit, a decision underscoring the assessment's importance and the fact that surveys can be critical tools for any department, not just Human Resources.

By segmenting the results by dozens of countries and hundreds of locations, the company is able to pinpoint any training and communication breakdowns, such as a location where numerous employees have not received the required CoC training. Moreover, Kimberly-Clark can identify risk factors, for example, when employees in a location indicate skepticism about follow-through by the company on reported violations or about fear of retaliation. Follow-up by the Internal Audit team can quickly address problems before they grow into major issues. There may be actual violations, or there may be situations in which employees believe a manager does not want to hear about problems (a message that managers can easily convey unintentionally). By taking the initiative with a broad-based survey, Kimberly-Clark manages its risk and safeguards compliance with the Code of Conduct, as well as with external regulations.

We created an Ethics Risk Assessment™ (ERA) to help leaders manage ethics. It is based on a six-factor model called B-CLEAR that helps identify high or low ethical risks (see the sidebar below). The 36-item tool captures elements of ethics that need to be managed to ensure that your organization is not only compliant but is creating a healthy ethical climate. Beliefs, Communication, Leadership, Equity, Awareness, and Rules/Regulations are each addressed by the ERA.

Even when ethical behavior is not mandated, it is expected by employees. Employees do not want to work for an unethical outfit, one that skirts the law. Most are ashamed of being part of such an enterprise. Sixty-six percent of Millennials agree working for a company that embraces and supports social responsibility is desirable; they seek such firms when job hunting.[5]

ETHICS RISK ASSESSMENT™ AND B-CLEAR MODEL

The Ethics Risk Assessment™ (ERA) examines employee attitudes and awareness of critical integrity and antifraud risks as part of a complete ethics program evaluation. It is based on the B-CLEAR model developed by Metrus Institute that covers Beliefs, Communication, Leadership, Equity, Awareness, and Rules/Regulations. Each of the six factors in the model reflects a key issue related to perception of ethics. The ERA measures employee perceptions and attitudes using 36 focused questions across the six B-CLEAR categories to provide guidance on how well the company is doing in meeting its compliance goals and where it needs to focus its training and communication efforts. The six categories combine to create a complete picture of the ethical culture of an organization. The categories and what they measure are the following:

Beliefs: *Embedded cultural standards and norms of behavior*

Attitudes regarding the company's values and how they relate to day-to-day work. Even employees with strong personal values are less inclined to take action and "do the right thing" if that is not part of the culture of the company.

Communication: *Unrestricted and fear-free downward, upward, and lateral communications*

How well managers create an environment that encourages open discussion of issues and how well they respond to issues when they arise.

continues

Leadership: *Belief that leaders can always be trusted to do the right thing*

How well managers set the right tone at the top and act consistently with the company's values and policies.

Equity: *Perceptions of justice, fairness, and consistency*

How well the company treats all of its stakeholders, both internal and external.

Awareness: *Education that goes beyond merely informing people of the rules*

How well the participants understand what is expected of them and how ethical behavior relates to their job and to the company's business goals.

Rules and Regulations: *Governance, formal systems, and processes that support ethical conduct*

Attitudes toward rules and regulations and whether they are effective in guiding behavior.

By using models such as B-CLEAR or similar approaches, an organization can fine-tune its focus from global ethics questions to specific components of ethics that can and should be managed to create a healthy and productive environment. These models also allow organizations to leverage limited training and communications funds by focusing on the areas generating the greatest risk while providing a measurement baseline for leaders to assess progress in meeting ethical goals. Finally, these models are crucial antifraud tools to capture how well the organization is creating an environment where employees feel secure enough to report potentially fraudulent activities.

Other measures in addition to surveys can be useful. Laura Mindek, founder of Mind*shift* Solutions and former Vice President of Worldwide Executive Development at American Express, relates,

"When the U.S. sentencing guidelines were new, I developed a program at Sony that became a model for prevention. One of the measures we used was a simple knowledge test tracked by individual employee and employee segments year-over-year. The government accepted it as a mitigating factor in determining fines."

Organizations must pay close attention to how senior management lives and models ethical behavior. This goes beyond financial irregularities. CEOs who verbally abuse others or executives who ignore policies and are never called to account set the tone for the whole organization. "I believe that 95 percent of an organization's ethics is comprised of the ethical behavior of top leadership and the other 5 percent is comprised of the practiced values of everyone else. And you get 90 percent of the 'everyone else's' ethical behavior from the example set by top leadership," remarks Howard Winkler of Southern Company.

Our life experience and attitudes predispose us to particular behaviors. Similarly, an organization's structures and systems will influence the behavior of its employees and leaders. For example, in the survey cited at the beginning of this chapter, almost one-third of the financial services executives reported feeling pressured by bonus or compensation plans to violate the law or to engage in unethical conduct. Often, there is not such clarity around the connections, and therefore a well-designed assessment of attitudes, perceptions, and behaviors can help us understand both the ethical character of the organization and where structural changes may be needed. With that understanding comes the potential to improve.

What is the return on such improvement? Is there "ROEB"—return on ethical behavior? The potential payback from measuring and managing ethical climate is significant. It is hard to count avoidance of scandal as a return, but certainly an enhanced reputation will benefit the corporate brand. A company with a solid ethical reputation will also be viewed more favorably by markets and investors. When co-workers behave ethically, greater trust will permeate the organization, and a high level of trust supports open, honest communication; better decision making; and individual accountability. Top candidates may be more attracted to the company, making recruitment and selection more efficient and more effective. The community and even the media will treat the ethical company differently from a company viewed as unethical or untrustworthy.

Action Tips

1. How well is your organization adhering to your corporate code of conduct? Do you have ready information to assess this question? If not, consider conducting an assessment to gauge awareness and to learn what employees' experience with the code and with reporting tools have been.

2. How well does your senior leadership model and promote your values? What is their view of themselves? How are they viewed by employees? Measure the difference in perceptions to raise executive awareness of how their actions drive the ethical climate.

3. To understand the ethics climate, consider a survey so that you can see ethical opinions across all major workgroups and teams. You may be surprised at the amount of variance across different groups.

Chapter 13
Diversity and Inclusion

"I can imagine nothing more terrifying than an Eternity filled with men who were all the same. The only thing which has made life bearable . . . has been the diversity of creatures on the surface of the globe."

— T. H. White, *The Book of Merlyn*

Organizations today realize that managing diversity and inclusion is not only a cultural value but also an essential component of adapting to the global, multicultural environment that is becoming the primary platform for business operations. Part of the challenge in managing diversity and inclusion is arriving at clear definitions of these concepts. Across many organizations, we see wide variation in how diversity and inclusion are defined.

From our experience, we recommend a broad definition of both concepts, such as the following:

- *Diversity:* Understanding, appreciating, and utilizing the differences among peoples for everyone's gain. This does not mean valuing differences for differences' sake. The benefits come from valuing people, regardless of their differences. Rather than focusing on demographic diversity (sex, race, tenure, age),[1] values diversity,[2] or job-related diversity (function, skills, goals, or information),[3] we like to include all individual differences because it affords an opportunity to recognize that individuals vary in what motivates them, the competencies they bring, their nonwork requirements, and so forth. We will talk more about this issue in the chapter on segmentation that follows in Section VII.

- *Inclusion:* "Inclusion is a sense of belonging: feeling respected, valued for who you are; feeling a level of supportive energy and commitment from others so that you can do your best work," according to Miller and Katz.[4] Mor-Barak and Cherin[5] defined inclusion as the extent to which individuals can access information and resources, are involved in workgroups, and have the ability to influence decision-making processes. Employees must be involved and included as part of the organizational family so that all have a sense of belonging and importance.

We have heard many employees—leaders included—talk primarily about diversity and inclusion as values that we should aspire to but seldom about the business benefits. As Darwin discovered years ago, diversity in our ecosystems and our genetics creates a stronger and more adaptable species. The same argument can be made regarding organizations. For example, an organization that has multicultural peoples of varying age, sex, cultural experiences, or other factors is more likely to detect trends in the marketplace that monocultural organizations may miss.

Some argue that diversity is not inherently advantageous. For example, much of our civilization's incredible agricultural productivity is a result of eliminating diversity with farmers all using just a few varieties of staple crops. True enough, but we regularly pay a price for monoculture when pests or disease sweep through and wipe out a growing season.

Consider NBA teams, which focus on talent, not diversity, for success. Few people would push player diversity initiatives as a strategy to win championships. Is that an effective argument against diversity? The reality is that most organizations do not have the narrow, unchanging strategic goals of a sports team, and many already have a diverse workforce—or will as demographic shifts continue. But diversity is not just a fact of life for modern organizations. We think of diversity as a resource to be tapped, a value we can realize through inclusion, and a potential competitive advantage for the firms that best capitalize on it.

Some long-standing businesses have demographic profiles consisting of mostly Generation X members and Baby Boomers with few Millennials. Their average tenure may be 15 or 20 years of service. In work we have done with these companies, we have found that these well-seasoned workforces know the ropes backward and forward. This is great for executing current operations, but with a generational monoculture they may risk missing new trends, not utilizing new tools that Millennials take for granted, and thus not achieving the full potential of the organization in the current environment.

Or consider two retail organizations, one in the United States and the other in Europe. Neither organization was interested in the trends or details of the others' market; in fact neither had a real understanding of the others' market. However, when a global player arrived on the scene with savvy employees in Asia, Latin America, Europe, and North America, it was able to connect more effectively with customers and to pick up emerging trends in one area of the world and transport them to other areas. Executives in this organization were culturally richer, enabling them to adapt and innovate faster than the more culturally limited firms. We will discuss innovation in Chapter 14.

Surveys and other measurement tools play a role in understanding how inclusive the organization is. The authors' experiences in measuring this area go back four decades, and they have incorporated their experiences and databases within the Metrus Institute. We find that four dimensions, which we abbreviate **B.E.S.T.**, capture many of the pertinent issues around the subjects of diversity and inclusion.

Balance and Respect

A key component of practicing diversity is ensuring your employees feel they are both valued and respected as individuals. In doing so, the organization can capitalize on what their workforce contributes by recognizing and utilizing the peerless talent each employee has to offer.

Employees must be provided with equal opportunities to learn, grow, and work in ways that maximize ACE. Remember, when ACE is high, everyone wins! Tailoring these opportunities to individual needs and abilities will add worth to the organization and make individual experiences more meaningful.

Effective Diversity Leadership

One of the most important factors for success with implementing diversity and inclusion includes the commitment of your organization's leadership. Management should be held accountable for both maintaining and executing diversity initiatives and for connecting them to business outcomes. If management does not support the organizational diversity effort, chances are neither will your employees.

Strategic Diversity Planning and Implementation

Having inclusion initiatives in place is an essential ingredient of your organization's success, but it is not sufficient. A strong foundation for inclusion is achieved by tying the inclusion values and goals to the overall business strategy. Employees must see the link between diversity/inclusion initiatives and organizational results. Business goals, policies, and procedures should both support and be consistent with diversity efforts.

Team Behaviors

You have heard the cliché "There is no I in team," but when talking about practicing inclusion, there is. For employees to feel as though they are part of a team, they must first feel valued and respected as *individuals*. Thus, employees must believe that their individual efforts, perspectives, and styles are welcomed within the team and that they add merit to team projects.

Each of these areas can be assessed with surveys and focus groups. Surveys provide pinpoint measures that allow leaders to compare how various groups respond to different questions. This comparison enables leaders to identify which groups may be feeling disenfranchised or less favorable on a particular issue.

Advanced analytics (see Chapter 6) can also tell us about differences in the relative significance of issues for distinct groups. In a global financial services company we found the drivers of Engagement were quite different for employees in Asia compared to North America and Europe (we discuss the reasons for this pattern in Chapter 6). Table 13.1 compares the top three drivers by region. Understanding and acting on what is most valuable to various groups demonstrates respect as well as awareness.

In one energy company that had taken diversity issues for granted, results from its first ever analysis of survey data by ethnicity were a real eye-opener. Figure 13.1 shows that not only did minorities have a different perspective on issues of diversity and inclusion as practiced in the company, but they had much less favorable responses regarding career opportunities and performance management.

Focus groups with the identified subgroups are a great tool to investigate these issues further. In the energy company, a series of focus groups with specific ethnic groups and some of mixed composition revealed the depth of concerns around inclusion and how those affected minorities' view of their future with the company. The belief that advancement and good reviews had a lot to do with social networks and visibility (to senior leaders) led many to the conclusion that long-term success was going to be an uphill battle. With a series of changes to promotion and performance systems, plus enhanced training for managers, the company was able to diminish the gaps over several years. Interestingly, a separate "diversity value" was not

Table 13.1 Drivers of Engagement in a Financial Services Company

North America	Asia	Europe
1. Professional Growth	1. Change Management	1. Professional Growth
2. Diversity and Inclusion	2. Senior Leadership	2. Diversity and Inclusion
3. Ethics	3. Work/Life Balance	3. Compensation

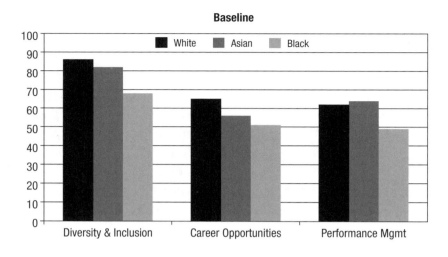

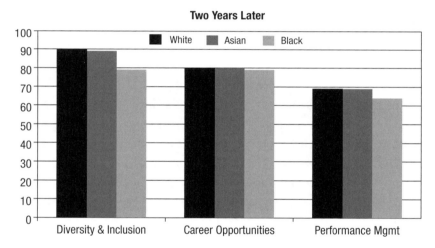

Figure 13.1 Ethnicity Differences in an Energy Company

part of the solution. In fact, if many organizations truly live their values, they will probably be inclusive by default.

Action Tips

1. Define diversity broadly to encompass as wide a range of individual differences as possible. Focus on inclusiveness

with the intent of recognizing the individual and unleashing the potential of all employees.

2. Where possible, use advanced analytics to examine differences among subgroups. The ability to link survey findings to the organization's HR databases can add significant value here.

3. Use the B.E.S.T. dimensions to ensure that your survey captures a range of diversity and inclusion issues.

Chapter 14

Innovation

"Capital isn't so important in business. Experience isn't so important. You can get both these things. What is important is ideas. If you have ideas, you have the main asset you need, and there isn't any limit to what you can do with your business and your life."

—Harvey Firestone, Founder of the Firestone Tire and Rubber Company

Today, innovation is sought in all walks of organizational life, not just in R&D. How can we innovate to improve existing business processes? Can we deliver more for less? Can we adapt our products and services (both to the end customer as well as along the supply chain) to deliver more value? Can you leverage your time more effectively? Are we creating products that the customer was not thinking about previously—the next iPod or Facebook, for example—that can bring in new revenue streams and customers? Does our business strategy depend on us out-innovating the competition (think Apple) in a particular industry? Is our supply chain innovation giving us a competitive advantage (think Walmart)?

Innovation definitions typically assume some amount of creativity in ideation or idea generation. It is not all ideation in an empty white room! Much innovation occurs at the work station and is definitely not limited to a particular department. Innovative companies talk about generating ideas from all corners and creating a climate that fosters innovation. Facebook did not come from a corporate R&D department. It came from a dorm room. Tamar Elkeles, VP of Learning and Organizational Development at Qualcomm observes, "We have to think about innovation in everything we do—how we recruit, how we manage performance, and how we reward and recognize people." Even organization design can have an impact; decentralizing control and putting more autonomy into regional and functional groups can energize innovation for some organizations.

Dyer and his colleagues, in examining over 3,000 executives and 500 individuals who had started innovative companies or invented new products, identified five characteristics that are often found in innovative people and organizations: questioning, observing, experimenting, networking, and associating.[1] They said that these are the characteristics of people like Apple's Steve Jobs, Amazon's Jeff Bezos, eBay's Pierre Omidyar, or P&G's A. G. Lafley. Although many of these characteristics will sound familiar, one of the toughest is associating—the ability to successfully connect seemingly unrelated questions, problems, or ideas from different fields. Dyer also concluded that the solution to many problems comes from outside the organization or even its industry: "We must aggressively and proudly incorporate into our work findings and advances which were not invented here."[2] This approach requires a culture that supports these behaviors with processes, rewards, and structures that enable them to happen.

Langdon Morris[3] proposed several provocative questions to start us thinking about measuring innovation:

- Are we targeting the right parts of our business for innovation?
- Can we change as fast as our markets do?
- Are we flexible enough?
- Is our strategy clear enough that we can translate it into innovation initiatives?
- How well do our strategies match with the way the market is evolving? (For example, if the industry is moving rapidly into technology, does your organization have the requisite technology expertise?)
- Do we have an effective innovation dashboard?

How Do Surveys or Other Assessments Help?

Whereas organizations that have chosen a distinct innovation strategy often ask more questions on an employee survey or conduct separate surveys of innovation, almost all organizations (and certainly all that use the ACE framework that includes Innovation as one of the five key drivers) capture some aspects of innovation in their broad employee surveys. Employees (or contractors, suppliers) can provide feedback on elements of the innovation process—on what is and is not happening.

Various aspects of creating an innovative organization can be captured via surveys or focus groups:

- Innovation process, such as idea generation and creativity, idea maturation and flow, and idea adoption
- Climate for innovating, such as willingness to take risks and strategic clarity around innovation
- Connection to the customer

In the first area above, questions can capture whether new ideas are sought and how people see creativity taking place. And even if organizations are adept at generating new ideas, can they translate these ideas into action? CEO Kathleen Flanagan of Abt Associates shared, "I believe in asking people at every level of the organization for their input."[4] Howard Schultz, CEO of Starbucks, says "I want big thinkers. I want people who are going to be entrepreneurial. . . . I want people to challenge the status quo."[5] If you fail to generate sufficient new ideas, the rest of the innovation process falls apart.

Organizations such as IBM, Coromandel, or Menasha talk a good deal about creating the right climate to support innovation processes.[6] For example, they and others ask if they have created an experimental and nonjudgmental environment where ideas are hatched. Are ideas shared openly or hoarded by silos? Is there a fair and transparent process for evaluating ideas that encourages future ideas? Are ideas rewarded—not only the ones that reach full implementation? Is there healthy competition to find new opportunities?

Is it a climate of recognition for challenging the status quo? Answers to these questions can tell you about the real level of support for innovation.

Coromandel, India's third-fastest-growing company with revenues of about $2 billion and over 7,000 employees in 509 locations, needed to find new ways to innovate in the manufacture of fertilizers, specialty nutrients, crop protection products, and retail products. It began with an innovation readiness assessment that enabled it to prepare leaders and determine the best roadmap to begin its journey to innovation.[7] The results are impressive. Ideas that made it through Coromandel's process have a net present value of nearly $1 billion.

As concluded at a recent Thought Leaders Retreat hosted by the SHRM Foundation,

> "Innovative companies do not only have an 'innovation department.' They have cultures, processes and systems where innovation occurs throughout the organization. HR can play a key leadership role in creating an innovative culture and in putting systems in place to drive innovation."[8]

Tine Huus, Organizational Development Manager at Nokia, notes that when the climate does not strongly support innovation, technology companies are at significant risk. They may find "employees innovating outside the company, in frustration channeling their creativity to private outside-of-work activities. This is a particularly dangerous pattern for high-tech companies. Employees get their kicks elsewhere!"

Finally, innovation will ultimately exist (or not) in the eyes of the customer. Employee surveys with innovation questions can be further segmented to look at the views of those closest to the customer. For example, in Figure 14.1 we show the answers to an innovation question by different employee segments. The sales people are far more skeptical that the company is generating new ideas that provide value to customers than those in the R&D group and the marketing group.

Question: Our company continuously innovates to bring new value to the customer

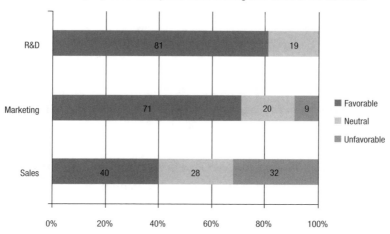

Figure 14.1 Response to Innovation Question by Three Groups

Of course, the ultimate arbiter is the customer. Customers should be surveyed or interviewed to learn more about their view of the organization regarding innovation, if this is a distinct area of intended competitive advantage. This feedback can also be helpful in understanding how new ideas, services, and products have an impact on the customer's value chain. Was our new product a game changer, like the iPod? If pricing changes were involved (think Kindle in black and white vs. color), were those offerings or tradeoffs worth the price (the value question)? Sometimes, innovation by a fast-follower is more successful than it is for a first-mover. Apple did not invent music players, the MP3 format, or smartphones, but the design genius behind the look and user interface of their products became a major factor in making Apple the most valuable company in the world.[9]

Marisa Harris observed that during her tenure at Citicorp, surveys and interviews with high net worth international and domestic clients showed that the company was weak in innovation. A group was created to design a new product that would make Citicorp be seen as sexy and exciting. The result was "Investing in Fine Arts with Citibank," a product that became successful after collaboration with many internal and external stakeholders. It is an example of the importance of creating enthusiasm and buy-in among both internal and external customers; without them great ideas often struggle to see the light of day.

But not all innovation is visible to the end customer. Innovative cultures create substantial innovation along the supply chain and in new ideas that the customer only sees in pricing—because the organization is leaner and can lower costs—or perhaps in quality enhancements—such as small increments in battery life on one of your mobile devices. Innovation can still create major value for the organization that results in lower costs, higher quality, reduced stress, or other intangible benefits. In the past, Toyota's production innovations meant the labor hours to produce a car were almost 10 percent lower than GM's: 31 hours vs. 34 hours. Those few hours translated to an annual cost difference of $1.8 billion dollars across an equal number of units.

Any survey or similar assessment tool should be complemented by strategic or tactical scorecard metrics associated with innovation, such as counts of actual ideas generated (and perhaps dollar value or another way to classify them), ideas tested, ideas adopted, and the resulting impact in terms of money, time, quality, and the like.

Most organizations are better at identifying ideas than they are at implementing them, although a contrasting risk is implementing ideas that are not aligned with the strategy. For example, a former financial services manager described an acquisition expected to produce diversified products. Though the new parent provided the resources to create new products, a lack of alignment of their two strategies resulted in many false starts at considerable expense.

The questions in Table 14.1 are designed to help develop a strategic framework for innovation and measurement of innovation. A team can be assembled to consider these questions at an early phase in an innovation improvement process.

Our experience suggests that by using a combination of survey, focus group, and hard innovation data embedded in a strategic framework, you can capture a great deal of information about the effectiveness of your innovation.

Table 14.1 Questions for Developing a Strategic Framework for Innovation

- How well do you generate new ideas that relate to revenue growth?
- How well do you generate ideas related to increased efficiency, productivity, or cost reduction?
- How effective are you in incubating and evaluating new ideas? Do you have criteria for evaluating ideas that balance idea generation versus becoming overwhelmed and unfocused? Criteria that are too stringent will stifle creativity, whereas criteria that are too lax with pull you off course.
- How effective is your organization at implementing new ideas? Once incubated and evaluated, is there a clear process for getting a new ideas to the goal and expected benefit?
- Do you have measures in place that help you manage this process and evaluate the outcome of new ideas (for example, savings, new products, revenue extensions)?
- Do you close the loop with employees, clearly communicating the disposition of ideas and suggestions? Are they told the what, when, and why, or is there a black hole for innovative ideas?

We have talked about using a variety of surveys to manage values—safety, ethics, diversity, innovation—in this section, in addition to the prior discussion about talent management and employee surveys. We picture a survey manager somewhere feeling overwhelmed by how to do all this. In Section VII, we will address how those can be rationalized in many cases into a more compact process that does not overburden the organization. In the next section will turn to the role of measurement in managing environmental constituents, described in the model in Chapter 1.

Action Tips

1. Does your strategy support innovation and the appropriate level of risk taking? Do you take steps to ensure that employees feel enabled to take appropriate risks?

2. Jatin DeSai, co-founder of innovation focused DeSai Group, related, "You already have many innovators in your organization, but they are hiding due to lack of an innovation-eco system."[10] Measure the climate for innovation via surveys, and examine the results across departments to verify that innovation is not being suppressed in any group. When you obtain low innovation scores in particular units that surprise you, dig deeper by meeting with employees or conducting a focus group to identify why innovation is slim.

3. Use simple and direct language with employees around proposed innovations, emphasizing outcomes: "Yes, we can do

this, and this is when you can expect to see it happen," and "No, we can't do that, and here is the reason why." In the absence of this kind of direct communication for understanding, employees are left wondering what happened, and they are less likely to offer their good ideas in the future.

4. Bring together a cross section of people in the organization to discuss the key stages of innovation described in the chapter and to test how they play out in your organization.

VI

MANAGING ENVIRONMENTAL CONSTITUENTS

One of the key stakeholder groupings described in Chapter 1 (see Figure 1.1) is environmental constituents. These stakeholders are external to the organization and often include unions, community leaders, environmental groups, and government entities. These groups need to be managed like all others, and effective strategy implementation hinges on building solid relationships with them. Our simple rule of thumb: Put a group on your radar if that group can affect your success. To manage or partner with those groups, you need good measures to understand their expectations, priorities, and actions.

For purposes of this book, we focus on two areas frequently asked about in terms of measurement. The first area focuses on labor relations. This area can range from the desires of organizational leaders to remain union free to building effective partnerships with bargaining groups. Expectations, approaches, and regulatory issues play out differently across the globe, but some fundamental measurement aspects can help in making sound decisions.

The second area is sustainability, which is not simply about environmental issues but about taking actions that will create sustainable financial performance, social responsibility, and environmental health. Sustainability requires managing many different stakeholders, ranging from employees (who play a major role) to green groups to regulatory agencies such as environmental protection agencies to social organizations and ultimately shareholders. We will also address the issue of employee volunteerism and its influence on success in the sustainability area.

Chapter 15

Using Information to Optimize Labor Relations and Union Outcomes

"Managers get the unions they deserve."
—Labor Arbitrator

Many organizations have a strong commitment to remain union free whereas others with union representation seek to create a productive and beneficial relationship. In either case, positive labor relations are essential. Though unions have traditionally polled their members on a variety of traditional bargaining issues such as pay and benefits, they are using surveys more effectively today to better understand their constituents. We will examine how surveys and other assessments can play a role in unionizing or in managing labor relations.

Union Representation

In a classic study, Getman and his colleagues identified some of the factors that lead to and predict successful unionization, including employee satisfaction, attitudes toward unions, behaviors during prior union elections, and wages.[1] Heneman and Sandver also performed a meta-analysis of the factors that predict the outcome of union certification elections, confirming that factors such as employee satisfaction with the organization is an area that is most controllable by management, compared to propensity to like unions, for example.[2] Factors such as fair treatment, open communication, job security, pay and benefit fairness, safe working conditions, and treatment with respect are often prominent in decisions about whether to vote for union representation. These factors have endured over many years because they represent issues that cause employees to support union representation.

Earlier in the book, we described three levels of employee engagement: basic satisfaction, commitment (role and organization), and advocacy. Advocacy is often seen as the pinnacle of Engagement, resulting in higher discretionary effort, greater volunteerism, and advocating on behalf of the organization to others. However, the recent recession once again taught us that the basics of satisfaction are not to be ignored; when employees are insecure, endure poor working conditions, see pay and treatment as unfair, and experience stifled communications, conditions are ripe for employees to look to a third party for relief. Employees are less focused on development, greater commitment, more teaming, and sharing when they are worried about the basics.

By knowing these factors, organizations can use a survey to identify the risks of becoming organized by a union.[3] Some organizations include these elements in their annual employee survey, often reported as a labor relations index. This practice makes eminent sense if your industry or job groups have been subject to unionizing in other arenas—especially if you have had previous attempts at union organizing. If you do not conduct a regular employee survey, administering a short employee relations survey to determine the health of the organization is feasible. These surveys can be as short as 15 questions, addressing such areas as being treated with respect, fair administration of pay and benefits, working conditions, and communications.

Although analysis of many surveys is focused primarily on the percentage of favorable ratings, employers should examine unionization surveys for the percentage of unfavorable ratings. For example, you could include an item on job security that scores 55 percent favorable and 45 percent unfavorable, meaning that 45 percent are fearful of their job security. Another organization might have 55 percent favorable, 40 percent neutral, and 5 percent unfavorable. The latter is far less risky as a profile for unionizing than the former one. Here, only 5 percent have strong negative views.

In all cases, communication is essential. After the surveys are completed is the time for some targeted actions, beginning with the most disaffected groups. Actions may include modified focus groups to dig into the root causes. Perhaps in the first group above, with 45 percent negative ratings, one-half may be driven by recent job cuts and the other half by news in the community about jobs going to other countries. Knowing the root causes allows you to target the right corrective actions.

In all cases, caution should be exercised to ensure that you are in compliance with local or country legal requirements about the use of surveys or other interventions during an organizing process.

Managing Labor Relations

Another scenario is organizations that are already working with an existing bargaining unit.[4] Surveys and focus groups can be excellent tools for managing these relationships. We have worked with companies and unions in a variety of these settings with a few lessons learned. For example, one global service organization engaged two of the authors to identify survey indices that would predict the likely outcome of contract ratification across 50 different regions. Using predictive analytic tools, we were able to identify fewer than 10 questions that predicted (with a great deal of reliability) the outcome of contract ratification votes. The organization has used this tool for over twenty years. It was best used to identify which units had the highest risk so the company could effectively campaign in those regions, uncover root cause problems, and solve issues before the next election. Predictive analytic tools are helpful when there may be different and even conflicting viewpoints among various locals and a national or global union.

Another use of surveys and focus groups is in coaching and developing leaders. Once organizations understand which regions have the highest and lowest labor relations risks, best practices learned in the low-risk regions can be adapted and applied to the high-risk ones. Though every unit may have different local issues, our experience suggests that these types of tools provide great insight that can be used to avert unnecessary labor strife.

Unions are also becoming savvier about the use of survey information. In the last century, information was often hoarded and not shared—information was viewed as "power." Unfortunately, in numerous cases we witnessed, union leaders were not always on a sound footing with the majority of their members, especially at the local level. A local leader might take a hard position that membership did not fully back, leading to difficult contract negotiations.

Today, we see enlightened leaders—both management and union—using survey information to focus on important issues and to make trade-offs that can work for both groups. If a union represented a highly stressed nursing group, for example, that strongly desires more predictable shift assignments, it may trade scheduling flexibility for perhaps a pay or benefit gain. Or a group that has not received pay increases for some time may be willing to make changes to increase productivity in some way. When used properly, surveys can be a great tool to direct management and labor to the right issues.

Such tools should not be used only defensively to avert a strike or avoid a union; they should be used for positive employee relations. The days of picking a fight are over, as witnessed by the United Auto Workers and Detroit's long adversarial history leading to a lack of global competitiveness. When management acts as if it will be negotiating in good faith with a union, and therefore acts to create positive employee relations, the results are usually rewarding: less stress and turnover, lower absenteeism, better safety, improved productivity and quality, and better customer outcomes. This is not an either-or—it is a why not!

Action Tips

Consider the following:

1. *If you are nonunion* and wish to remain so, do you have predictive labor relations indices to alert you to deteriorating

conditions that will make unionizing possible or even likely? Consider building in a regular labor relations check by adopting a labor index that you use as a stand-alone instrument or that you couple with an employee survey of other issues.

2. *If you are already unionized,* do you have a predictive labor relations climate index that can be used to gauge the mood of the workforce and the likely risks as you prepare for the next labor negotiation? Such an index can also provide positive employee relations practices that will create a stronger level of trust between management and employees.

3. *If you are union leader,* do you have survey tools that will help you gauge the sentiment of your membership? What are the most pressing issues, and what are members willing to trade off to obtain them?

Chapter 16

Using Measurement to Support Sustainability

"Success is not sustainable if it is defined by how big you become or by growth for growth's sake."[1]
—Howard Schultz, CEO, Starbucks

Sustainability, Community, and Volunteerism

Another major area in which surveys and measurement can play a role is volunteerism and sustainability. Sustainability today is no longer simply about being "green." The triple bottom line—financial, environmental, and social—represents a cluster of concerns that many organizations share in common with shareholders, communities, environmental groups, employees, and customers. Organizations such as Starbucks and Coca-Cola realize that their customers, employees, and suppliers are all part of creating a sustainable culture that can endure socially, environmentally, and financially. The treatment of sustainability and volunteerism has been the subject of many articles and books. Here we focus on how measurement can help in addressing these issues and opportunities.

Volunteerism

Though some volunteerism is related to environmental issues, volunteerism can occur in many different aspects of work and nonwork life. One of the things that we have observed over the years is that highly Engaged employees tend to volunteer more in many ways—for community activities, for environmental improvements, and for special assignments at work. Engaged employees are more energized and willing to put in additional contributions beyond the minimum, not only at work but in their life outside work.

As organizations adapt to a 24-hour cycle of integrated work and play, Engaged employees rise to the occasion in a variety of situations—their work, home, religious affiliations, hobbies, sports, and many other areas. Conversely, increased volunteerism can enhance engagement. One leader in a U.S. energy company noted, "Opportunities to volunteer in the community on behalf of the company can also build employee Engagement. It is a particularly useful tool in engaging very low and very high seniority employees for whom rapid career movement may be difficult."

Surveys and other assessment tools can provide feedback on employees' involvement in a host of these activities that pertain to the corporation and its interface with communities, such as going green. For years, companies like AT&T and IBM have encouraged their employees to be strong contributing members of their communities—to give back. These volunteer activities have also created a positive image for the organizations.

One oil company refinery realized that its role in a regional community was fragile; the community could make life miserable for the leaders of this operation. An environmental spill or negative oil company press could bring down a host of regulatory burdens that would make these leaders miss their corporate earnings objectives and even threaten their ability to do business in the community in which it operates. We worked with this company to create several key metrics in the corporate scorecard to capture environmental, community, and regulatory issues so that the top team had continual gauges to track this risk. Questions regarding environmental or community issues were integrated into an annual employee survey.

Additional target surveys, interviews, and focus groups with community members provided further information to create a risk index of how effective community relations were. These gave the organization an early warning signal of impending threats or opportunities. These measures were a constant counterbalance to pressures to reduce costs and to increase production output. By using a balanced set of metrics, some of which included survey indices and scored interviews, company executives were able to make tradeoffs that allowed them to successfully navigate challenging financial, values, and political goals.

Sustainability

The oil refinery example highlights the growing need to manage financial, environmental, and human capital sustainability. A United Nations Global Survey of CEOs in 2010 found that 93 percent of CEOs viewed sustainability as "Important" or "Very Important" to their companies, and 96 percent said it should be fully embedded in their strategy and operations.[2]

One major definition of sustainability is the triple bottom line that many organizations report in their annual reports or other communications:

- Sustainable earth, environment, and energy
- Sustainable social environment, including talent or human capital
- Sustainable profitability

We have discussed the second area, talent, throughout this book. By optimizing talent—creating high ACE—you build a strong reservoir of talent for today and tomorrow. The beauty is that the investment in talent to create high Alignment, Capabilities, and Engagement produces high ROI. High Alignment leads to better financial and operational performance; high Capabilities leads to improved customer loyalty and retention; and high Engagement leads to retention of good talent and a more active level of effort in the organization. Optimizing talent is a win-win for all. Employees see their personal skills portfolio being enhanced, and corporations gain longer-term commitment to the organization's success.

What is seldom discussed is the impact of employees on the other two sustainability areas introduced at the beginning of this chapter. Though other investments and actions are needed, employees properly focused (A), equipped (C), and engaged (E) can help the organization and their communities make major improvements in waste reduction, energy conservation, and reduced environmental risks. Sustainability pertains to all employees, but we have seen it of particular interest to younger generations.

According to a study done by TANDBERG and Ipsos MORI of 17,000 people in 15 countries, 81 percent of U.S. respondents surveyed said they would prefer to work for a company that has a good reputation for environmental responsibility.[3]

Take Starbucks as a case in point. The company found that it attracts employees as well as customers because of its values, including green policies and reputation. Starbucks buys organic beans from farmers on a fair-trade basis. Its policies are aimed at reducing environmental pollution, such as using coffee sleeves rather than double cupping.

This environmental commitment is a major source of talent and market advantage for Starbucks. The company did not wait for environmental stewardship to become commonplace but instead took the lead in making a statement to the world. These actions have enabled Starbucks to retain employees longer than competitors, to attract and keep customers, and to create sustainable profits.

The role of surveys and assessments is crucial to organizations in this arena. For example, Starbucks conducts regular surveys with its employees to test how well it is living its values. Customers have also been surveyed and interviewed to elicit their views—positive or negative—regarding the company's policies and approach to sustainability. By regularly surveying these groups, organizations have a better understanding of how well green policies, for example, are being implemented across many locations around the globe. Surveying enables the organization to quickly focus on regions or locations where adjustments are required.

Starbucks' Howard Schultz reemerged from his retirement as Chief Executive Officer when the company began to "lose its way." Schultz explained, "Turning around a culture is very difficult to do because it's based on a series of many, many decisions."[4] From market data and employee feedback, Schultz realized that the company had drifted from its original commitments espoused in its values and that the company needed a values overhaul to rediscover its roots.

Schultz and his team visited scores of stores, talked with associates and customers, and literally took a time-out, closing stores for an evening (a major statement for any retailer!) to re-communicate the vision and values and to commit to a renewed direction. The results have been impressive, with Starbucks again on a big growth curve after a significant hiccup. Schultz observed, "The relationship we have with our people and the culture of our company is our most sustainable competitive advantage."[5]

Starbucks is not alone. Many organizations, under the pressure of quarterly financial goals, drift slowly—the boiled frog syndrome—away from commitments that may require financial investments or precious time to maintain. Where is your organization today? A balanced scorecard approach can be a major tool to help organizations strike that balance between short-term results and long-term sustainability.

And feedback tools such as surveys, interviews, and focus groups can be a strong partner, when constructed well, to help organizations obtain crucial information related to sustainability.

Surveys can help both leaders and green advocates assess viewpoints and behaviors taking place both inside and outside the organization.

In this section, we have covered a variety of uses of surveys and other diagnostic tools to help leaders make myriad decisions that can provide competitive advantage or disadvantage. Managing sustainability will be an immense issue in the future, leading to our next section addressing some of the challenges looking forward.

Action Tips

1. Smart firms today build sustainability indices to help them take a proactive vs. reactive stance in areas such as green, community reputation, and regulatory relations. Do you have measures of sustainability?
   a. What about the sustainability of your workforce?

b. ACE can provide a rough surrogate for sustainability measures because it captures both the current and future value of the workforce, as we described in Chapter 4.

2. Consider including survey items in your overall employee survey dealing with sustainability and volunteer issues. You will need to gauge how important community relations are to your business. What is your reputation for sustainability in the marketplace? Will that reputation help or hinder you going forward as more eyes from interest groups, community members, and regulatory bodies examine how your organization behaves?

3. Have you done analytical work to determine the role that sustainability plays in attracting and retaining talent for your organization? Have you used advanced analytics to understand how volunteerism helps your organization and to identify the leading drivers of such volunteerism?

VII

PREPARING FOR THE FUTURE—NOW!

In the previous sections, we addressed the effective uses of employee and related surveys, along with other assessment tools such as 360s, focus groups, interviews, and polls. But what are the emerging opportunities for organizations to measure critical success factors in more strategic ways or to use measurement for speedy tactical decisions needed in a run-fast world? This section will address subjects that we hope will kick-start conversations in your organization. We will also offer a future template for your consideration, but keep in mind, in many parts of the world, the future is already here.

The first two chapters of this section will deal with the development of strategic decision measures needed to obtain intelligence from employees and a variety of other stakeholders. Executives and managers at every level require actionable information essential for meeting a variety of objectives, including detecting future risks and emerging threats, gaining insights into current problems, identifying new opportunities, and tracking key stakeholders.

The first chapter in this section focuses on broader models for capturing such actionable information. The second chapter focuses primarily on how to use the "eyes" of employees as the lenses for obtaining and using this information and outlines the three stages for building an employee intelligence system.

The third chapter will deal with the issue of employee segmentation—how to use information more effectively and efficiently to make decisions that are appropriate for smaller groups. In a world of increasing cost pressures, organizations will not have the luxury to deliver one-size-fits-all programs to every employee, no more than they would use all their marketing or advertising dollars equally across all consumer segments. This chapter will provide ideas and tools for thinking about how information can be made richer and can enable organizations to better focus the right resources on the right group. This perspective on employee segmentation also has implications for thinking about diversity in a broader way.

Chapter 17

Do You Have a Strategic Intelligence System?

"Where is the wisdom we have lost in knowledge? Where is the knowledge we have lost in information?"

—T. S. Eliot, *Choruses from the Rock*

The earlier sections of the book discuss the uses of surveys and other data-gathering tools to deal with current issues. But will those efforts be enough in today's marketplace? We only have to look to the faster-paced industries or economies to gain insights into what the rest of the world will be like in ten, five, or even fewer years. As one of our interviewees from a large retailer in Shanghai told us, its North American and European partners are not providing models, tools, or processes that work in China because their information and values do not fit the country's pace of change. When the average turnover of professionals is under 20 months, many labor models collapse.

Not only do labor models collapse, but so do supplier models and customer models. Technology has enabled a new level of customer delivery, and customer expectations have quickly evolved to incorporate the most advanced capabilities. Today you expect your auto dealer to instantly find the car you want in his network and to deliver it to you before you go to a competitor. We want faster transportation, speedy customer service, and quick checkouts at our retail stores. We often turn around survey results to our customers in days compared to months several decades ago; in fact, many customer or guest survey processes post near real-time results to the service provider. Models that assume static customer demands quickly become history.

The same is true for suppliers. They are not static. Supplier management demands are greater today because of what our customers expect. Firms that cannot manage suppliers with agility get squeezed in the middle, often resulting in inferior margins. Static models with long-term supplier agreements or cost-plus models are fading because they are not effective in dealing with fast-paced changes driven by the market and customers.

One major reason for the collapse of previous employee, customer, and supplier models is the speed of information needed to adapt processes or policies more quickly. If you have an early detection system for talent risk—for example, turnover of high performers—you can rapidly engage the risk-prone talent in effective ways to extend tenure with your firm. In a world of such frequent turnover, extending tenure by a year or even a few months can be a competitive advantage.

Another reason for the collapse of prior models is the quality of information. In the United States, turnover in retail can vary widely, with some firms incurring over 200 percent turnover annually. Obviously, this is a big cost. One southwestern retailer we worked with was able to reduce its turnover from over 150 percent to less than 100 percent—a big impact on the bottom line. Speedily obtaining the right decision information from employees, managers, and other sources enabled this retailer to more effectively identify the drivers of turnover and to target certain retail locations for support and store manager coaching to improve the drivers that allow company executives to reduce turnover rates.

Will your information be fast enough and of the right quality to be relevant? Will you be able to detect emerging trends in time to adjust? Will you be able to combine information that comes from various channels at different times in a way that will give you an advantage or help you avert a crisis? Will you be able to access and codify the right data among the mass of bytes competing for your attention?

These are a few of the questions that this chapter will address. We will discuss what leading firms are already doing and likely scenarios of what will be required, enabling better planning and investing in the right tools for tomorrow—today!

If you think about the space station, a war room, or a nuclear plant control room, then you are on the right track. These operations require pinpoint timing of relevant information. If a nuclear plant has leading indicators to inform the control room of ground disturbances that might indicate an earthquake, troubleshooters can take action from precautionary measures to a full shutdown if the quake seems imminent. One of the challenges in organizations today is that because they have more time to react than, say, the nuclear plant operator, they do not perceive the need to quickly address the early warning signs even though the customer or talent ground is already shaking.

Whereas we talked about strategic scorecards briefly in Chapter 2 and analytic uses of employee survey data in Chapter 6, in this chapter we will look at decision needs using the broadest lens. What is the totality and type of information—strategic and tactical—that will be needed in this new environment, and how can we design and manage such systems? This chapter is about holism as well as adaptability. We will bring back some of our key concepts described throughout the book, embedded in a holistic framework that we hope demonstrates living examples of this dynamic information environment and what you can do to prepare.

Are You Gathering and Analyzing the Right Information?

As we indicated in Chapter 2, having the right strategic indicators among the many possible dashboard gauges is imperative. Think about pilots and the speed at which their aircraft is moving. If something goes wrong with altitude or wind shear, they do not have much time to react. They need the few "right" gauges to focus their attention and then make split-second decisions. Schiemann and Lingle, in their book *Bullseye!: Hitting Your Strategic Targets Through High-Impact Measurement*, addressed this issue.[1] As they explained, an organization's scorecard should generally have no more than twenty strategic measures, balanced across financial, operational, people, customer, supplier, and environmental success indicators.

But as Schiemann and Lingle discovered, a balanced scorecard does not come out of thin air, nor should it be the dictate of the CEO or a tossed-together scorecard team. An effective scorecard requires a well-thought-out translation of the critical requirements of the overall business strategy—vision, mission, values, strategic goals, and crucial success factors—into meaningful metrics. One of the most effective tools we have found for doing that is to build a strategic value map (see example in Figure 17.1) to help everyone understand how value is created in your organization's business model.

We introduced a financial services firm map in Chapter 2. The organization has a long history and a dramatic turnaround story.[2] The strategy map (Figure 17.1, previously presented in Chapter 2) shows that to achieve the financial outcomes listed on the right side of the diagram, the executives of this firm need to manage the factors to the left of those financial outcomes. Those factors to the left drive or cause the financial results. For example, the leaders need to retain clients because the market niche is limited and the loss of a client is difficult to replace—a key driver of revenue and net income. These customer outcomes are influenced by customer drivers such as speed of response to loan requests (under Product/Service Value) or responsiveness (under Relationship Management). These in turn are driven by numerous People, Supplier, and Operational drivers further to the left in the diagram.

Each of the factors in the diagram requires a special measure that enables the factor to be managed effectively. This is a good example of the importance of recognizing the synergy of thinking about multiple stakeholders and measures in the design of our measurement system. More and more, we find that information portals and intelligence systems are becoming vital sources of the real-time information that makes the scorecard come to life. Portals should provide as close to real-time information as is cost-effective. The employee portal is typically the centerpiece of the framework because employees are managing the processes and stakeholders, and hence, have a great window on the other key elements required for success. We will address this topic in more detail in the next chapter.

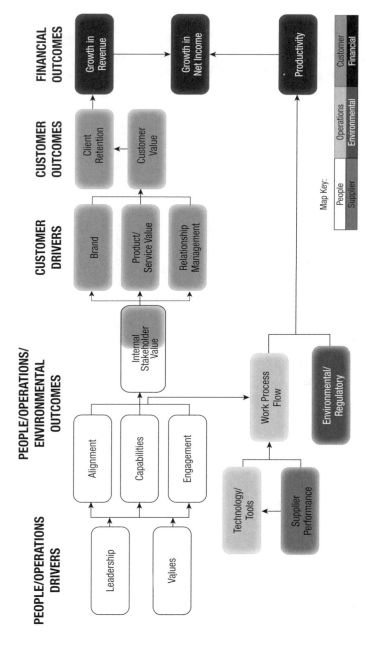

Figure 17.1 Financial Services Value Map[3]

Intelligence systems do not necessarily mean complex, costly, and high-technology investments. Much depends on the size of your firm. If you own a small service business, you may handle much of this information on a spreadsheet—the key is having it on your radar! The financial services firm initially obtained much of the information from a few suppliers and internal spreadsheets. Only later, after the company was convinced of the tool's utility, did it begin to automate some of the reporting.

Synergies in Measurement

A robust model generates many opportunities for measurement synergy. One such synergy is recognizing that the best way to measure a number of the concepts in the map is through surveys. To that end, the financial services firm engaged us to build indices (see Chapter 6) in a strategically designed survey (see Chapter 5) to help it assess some of the factors on the strategy map. By planning ahead, the company captured a number of its chief business drivers at the same time: values such as teamwork, Engagement, performance management as part of Alignment, and Leadership, for example, in Figure 17.1.

In addition, we were able to use an internal value assessment (IVA is described in Chapter 3) in conjunction with the employee survey during certain data collections to obtain internal customer value scores—a centerpiece of its strategy map. These value ratings that each of their departments such as Credit or Customer Service created were a major source of information on how well those departments were aligned in support of the overall company goals. In addition to obtaining client loyalty scores, a survey of clients was deployed on an annual basis, with periodic specialty surveys when needed. The surveys were designed to capture reactions to new policies or products.

Careful design of the data collection for these various measures enabled us to synthesize and analyze information coming from internal customers, client, and employee portals into a more coherent whole. For example, one such analysis identified the Customer Service function as a bottleneck in the value chain. Data from the client survey pointed to speed and responsiveness gaps. Data from the internal service survey showed internal customer concerns with responsiveness, Capabilities to deliver quality service, and coordination of deliverables with other departments. Finally, data from the employee survey showed lower Engagement scores in this group and declining ratings of Alignment, recognition, and supervision. These data allowed senior leaders to sit down with the manager of this group and create a plan for his personal development to address supervisory skills, provide enhanced team training, and make changes in processes that eliminated the bottlenecks from this group in the value chain.

Another critical gating item was speed of response to loan requests. At the time, having wait times of three days or more for loan requests was not uncommon. By analyzing data from multiple sources, the organization was able to reduce its response time to 24 hours by changing loan review processes and by increasing employee alignment. This modification required changes to response time of credit information from suppliers, changes in the Credit department's decision processes, and improvements in alignment and competencies of people in both Credit and Account Management. By streamlining—really aligning—the organization behind this goal, this firm was able to retain more clients who purchased even more loans from the company. Once again, information coordinated through multiple information portals helped in this decision process.

What about Important Tactical Drivers?

Subordinate to the critical scorecard metrics that we have discussed is a broader number of tactical measures that should be aligned with the strategic ones. These might include measures of hiring effectiveness, customer service wait times, supplier on-time performance, communications effectiveness, and so forth. The key point here is carefully selecting the right indicators to provide the best early warning system and evaluation of progress toward the organization's goal.

You might ask, "What about the department goals for groups such as Training, IT Programming, or Accounts Receivable?" Are they lost?

No, they are simply more tactical and need to be addressed at a different level. Every group needs to have key performance indicators, or KPIs, that are aligned with the overall scorecard, but the senior team does not need to drill down to those measures unless something in its overall strategic indicators signals a concern. This approach keeps the senior team doing strategic work, and allows departments to manage their affairs with minimal micromanagement. So yes, there will be tactical measures at the department, team, and individual level, and each of these levels should have a critical few measures that help them manage to goals aligned with the organization.

To manage progress toward goals, information must flow rapidly at the right time. Obtaining feedback on a downturn in employee engagement 18 months after it is has happened means that you are like a pilot without an altitude indicator in your plane for a long time, relying on luck rather than on fact. Though visual is great, when you hit a cloud patch, the game may be over! We knew one firm that had developed a schedule of surveying its employees every two years, sometimes three. What was their logic? They did not see satisfaction or engagement change rapidly, and once they received the survey findings, it took them about two years to implement improvements.

Breaking down the organization's process, its survey vendor took six to eight weeks to return survey feedback; the senior team took another one to two months to sit down and review it, and the management team took another two to three months to figure out priorities. Their data were already over six months old and most likely stale. The firm then had a study team investigate those issues further, and finally after about 10 to 12 months, it took some action. Needless to say, the company was losing altitude rapidly, and by the time it attacked the core issues, many employees felt that the actions were too little too late.

Compare this scenario with a company in which data could be reported back to the leadership team in one week after the survey, and the team made decisions on company-wide priorities within two weeks. Managers throughout the organization had their data within two weeks and were working on action plans. Real change began happening in the second month after the survey!

Averting Crises

Consider Coheal,[4] a health care firm that was in a sales crisis. The sales numbers were diving, and members of the leadership team were trying to figure out how they got there. The deteriorating situation had occurred without any leading indicators to help it avert the crisis. The best West Coast sales representatives with the most lucrative clients and the greatest longevity had just left to work for a competitor for higher salaries, following a beloved sales manager who had left over a year ago. Although turnover was deemed an important balanced scorecard indicator for this organization because of the impact on long-term customer relationships, it was a lagging indicator after much damage had already occurred. This situation could have been foreseen and perhaps prevented.

When our team was called in, we found that no leading indicators were being tracked. The firm's employee values survey was insufficient as a leading indicator. It had a few items that might have indicated trouble, but it was not organized into an index or tool that could be watched before people walked out the door. The company was missing some necessary items that predict likely turnover.

Furthermore, the company's exit data were flawed and incomplete. Not every HR rep participated in exit interviews, and fewer still wrote up complete information on the causes of turnover or other facts that might help the case. And no one had analyzed the information to look for trends. Sadly, in hindsight, many of the reasons for leaving, given in exit interviews, were bogus: That everyone had left for family or personal reasons or that nobody had a problem with a supervisor or management was hard to believe.

When we talked to the West Sales VP, we received vague answers that told us she did not really know what was driving this trend—perhaps the compensation was not enough, or reps were being asked to do too much. Interestingly, other regions were not experiencing these issues.

Ironically, some of the relevant data were there but were not captured in the right way or in time to make a difference. For example, a sales manager left and then recruited a good rep six months later, and a blowup had occurred at a regional sales meeting, but no action had been taken. One important item in the existing survey—intentions to stay with the company—had shown a decline in the last cycle. Also, an item on being treated with respect had declined in the disaffected region. Write-in comments on the survey indicated that pay was not competitive with other firms. Moreover, comments submitted to the company's "electronic suggestion box" from this region described a lack of updated tools and administrative work that consumed an increasing amount of sales time. The message was there, although fainter than it might have been with the right tools.

If you were to think about a more insightful measurement system, you might do the following:

- *Set up leading indicators.* A regular survey of the workforce, and in particular the high performers, would have signaled a red flag a long time ago.
- *Make sure the right questions are in the survey.* Some questions are great for predicting turnover, others for ethics or innovation, and so forth. In this case, we would have wanted items dealing with pay relative to effort, fairness, goal expectations, communications, and the like. Chapter 9 includes an in-depth review of items that are good predictors of turnover.
- *Balance inexpensive survey information with regular focus groups* to test the waters and to delve more deeply into issues identified in the survey. Focus groups might have probed in greater depth the fiasco at the regional meeting or the challenges the reps found in their market. A few individual interviews following this event might have been helpful to discuss supervisory issues.
- *Look from the outside in.* How did customers in that region feel? Perhaps customers already saw the strains in their relationships with the reps, or perhaps they demanded services or information the reps could not produce. Besides sales numbers, regular customer surveys or interviews help ensure that the customer is not withdrawing over time; they

can also reflect internal problems such as insufficient information or resources or the attitudes of the reps.

- *Fix the exit interview process* to obtain more useful information and to make certain that the process is adhered to. We recommend gathering additional exit information between three to nine months after an employee has left, as mentioned in Chapter 9. This time frame allows for more accurate information and better comparison to talent competitors.
- *Make sure that the information gathered will help with trend analysis and decision making.* Also, analyze the data in a way that will be useful, thinking about which turnover causes are controllable or not.
- *Have tools to integrate issues* raised in your suggestion boxes or other information vehicles into a common framework.
- *Automate data collection* as much as possible, or leverage through third parties.
- *Gain a commitment from your senior leaders* that they and managers they oversee will hold themselves accountable for the results and for improvements.

In the next chapter we will focus primarily on the employee intelligence system because it is the centerpiece of so much information that flows through employees.

Action Tips

1. Do you have the information portals and intelligence systems needed to manage in today's fast-paced, competitive environment? Consider the following:
   a. Do you have ready information when quick decisions are needed? Try making a list of decisions that your organization has made over the past three to six months. How confident are you that the information allowed you to make the optimal decision? If you were queasy about the decision, what information would have helped?

    b. How many times in the past year has someone had to rush off and spend inordinate time looking for information on a pivotal issue, such as turnover, customer issues, quality, or safety? If often, then you may need better measures built in to track major issues.

    c. Have you been able to draw insightful business conclusions by *coordinating* information from customers, employees, suppliers, and other sources of data? For example, in the area of sustainability, how prepared is your organization to become more sustainable in profit, people, and environmental outcomes? These areas require information across different stakeholder groups.

2. Conduct an audit of all your measures being used in the organization. Sort them into two categories. For each measure, list what decisions are made with that measure.

    a. Place the measures for which you cannot readily identify decisions into a Challenge grouping.

    b. Place the others in a Decisions Made grouping. For each of these, rate the level of importance the decision made to your organization's success. You can then make judgments about the relative worth of that information.

3. Do you have a strategy value map to help everyone see the big picture? See the Action Tips at the end of Chapter 2 for more suggestions.

4. Do you have a balanced scorecard to focus resources and management attention—keeping management at a strategic level? See Schiemann and Lingle's *Bullseye!: Hitting Your Strategic Targets Through High-Impact Measurement* for more details on how to design and implement balanced scorecards.

Chapter 18

The Employee Intelligence System

"When everything is intelligence—nothing is intelligence."
—Wilhelm Agrell, University of Lund, Sweden

An employee intelligence system (EIS) is a systematic way for capturing, storing, and synthesizing strategic and tactical information from employees for a variety of purposes. When we talk about employees, also think about contractors, part-timers, interns, or outsourced labor. They too may have invaluable information that can be gleaned. An EIS includes three key features:

- A systematic process for gathering strategic or tactical information that will be available for all relevant stakeholders
- A storage place for information that may be relevant now or in the future
- Processes for synthesizing data into information and for converting information into knowledge for important organizational decisions

One major difference of the EIS approach compared with organizations that conduct scores of surveys and other assessments is its *integrated design*, anticipating both what information is likely to be relevant and how that information might be connected to decisions. While existing HR information systems (HRIS) include huge amounts of employee data, rarely have they included the smart systems that will bring those data to life.

Another distinguishing quality of EIS is its holism, crossing traditional functional information silos to look at the whole rather than suboptimizing the parts. Also, this approach is likely to be more cost-effective per decision in the long term than traditional approaches. Rather than thinking about all the various survey and measurement needs as separate initiatives or pieces of data, the EIS approach instead provides intelligent capture of strategically prioritized employee data, integration of those data into meaningful information, and a system for utilizing such information on a timely basis.

To create an EIS, three steps are important: design, synthesis, and integration. We will now take a look at each.

Design

The key to building an effective EIS is good design. The best designs start with the business and talent strategies in mind and with creation of a framework for how this information will best be obtained. The goal is to wisely plan and schedule information collection so that it is both efficient and effective in providing needed information at the right time. Questions to be asked at this stage include the following:

- What are the three to six human capital priorities in our strategic or talent plans?
- Do we have sufficient measures in each of these areas to provide guidance in executing these plans?
- How will we obtain and coordinate these measures?
- What information from employees will provide input to understand needs (needs analysis), provide feedback on execution, and serve as leading indicators of desirable outcomes (such as retention of pivotal people, customer loyalty, or productivity)?

For example, if retention of top performers is a talent goal, we would identify the appropriate measures that capture not only talent turnover but also leading indicators that will give us early warning signals of impending breaches. Additionally, we would want root cause information, which is likely to be obtained and codified from post-exit interviews or questionnaires. In our new future, this information might also be garnered from Internet postings to our alumni site or from special alumni polls.

If the business is global, we would want that information captured on a timely basis, perhaps more frequently in priority regions (perhaps Asia if we are expanding there) or for vital jobs (perhaps sales representatives) or for high-risk locations (perhaps Shanghai and Singapore if retaining talent is more precarious there). The best data might be employee survey information that captures predictors of retention, integrated with exit data and interview data from former employees (particularly in high-turnover locations).

If we are losing hires in key jobs in the early stages of affiliation, we may also want tracking data that target information from these groups, such as hiring and onboarding survey feedback or pulse surveys taken at 7, 30, 60, and 90 days.

A key part of the design will be thinking carefully about how these data will be coordinated with the other priority areas identified in the questions above. For example, if ethics is a major priority area and one of the factors to track and report to your board, employee survey information collected on a timely basis coupled with ethics hotline information and operational data might be helpful.

Organizations such as Starbucks and other retailers, for example, not only look to employee perceptions of ethical risks but also track sales ratios and store performance. If a store begins to drop in revenue during certain shifts, someone on those shifts might be dipping into the till. The coordination of the survey data in a timely fashion with the above retention survey is an opportunity to save cost on data capture and to coordinate information across these areas when useful.

You may be feeling a bit overwhelmed by all the information presented, which brings us to a key point. Data are becoming cheaper. Even converting data to information for decision making is becoming less expensive when it is *designed in* to the process. We do not want you to be drawn into enormous data management tasks—instead, we value targeted information that is readily available when needed.

Therefore, we advise creating not only a framework for data management but also decision rules—preferably automated—that will focus your efforts on only those issues that require your attention. Table 18.1 provides an example of how an organization can combine employee survey information—often the best leading indicator of ensuing issues—with other forms of information to arrive at decisions about whether corrective action is needed. This EIS is a ready source of information to make rapid decisions to intervene, for example, if red flags appear in ethics, retention, or safety that might sidetrack the company, increase costs, and threaten the brand.

Additional discussion of the design of employee surveys is addressed in Chapter 5.

Analysis of Data into Information

Though bits of survey and other data can quickly become overwhelming, they can be managed in two ways. First, do not collect hoards of data that will cloud thinking and distract focus. If your organization is planning to downsize in significant ways over the next few years, job security questions are probably not going to add a lot of value unless you need to retain targeted groups.

One financial organization with which we worked had tons of data in storage. They collected everything they could because the

Table 18.1 Integrating Data within an EIS

Driver	People Equity Factor	Survey Source	Additional Data Source
Retention	Engagement	Employee	Exit data Post exit interviews
Ethics	Alignment	Employee	Hotline Hotline department interviews
Safety	Alignment	Employee	Safety incidents Lost-time accidents
Leader Effectiveness	Capabilities	360	Employee Ratings Unit ACE scores
Brand	Capabilities	Employee	Offer turndown surveys College surveys

cost of collection was diminishing. However, the amount of data was debilitating. So much information was being reported out to everyone that people started deleting reports coming from this group. Sadly, some managers tried to digest it all, wasting enormous amounts of time. Decide what is worthwhile for both today and during the time window of your strategic plan—for example, three years.

Second, once you have information, categorize it into meaningful chunks. For surveys, for example, you might group questions into indices such as a union predictor index, safety index, leadership index, Engagement, and so forth. We like the ACE framework because we can create A, C, and E indices that are predictive of many things that organizations care about—productivity, customer loyalty or retention, operating performance, or turnover. Moreover, the A, C, and E factors also have many drivers that can form indices predictive of such factors as unionization, ethics, diversity, quality, or accidents.

Another level of synthesizing is to combine information from several data sources into valuable information. Many organizations do this regularly with 360 evaluations of employees. Other examples might be a Functional 360™ that we conduct at Metrus. It includes a 360-degree look at functional excellence. This concept was introduced in Chapter 3. Views from users, employees, *funders*, and *influencers* (peer-function leaders who interface with the function) can be combined into an overall view of effectiveness or into specific indices of aspects of excellence, such as service excellence, product impact, or product awareness. Synthesizing such information into valuable information packets enhances the value of the data collected and enables more effective decision making.

For example, a forward-thinking pharmaceutical chief security officer (CSO) we worked with realized that his unit was seen as overhead and that the organization and his unit would continue to have cost pressures. How could he ensure that those cost decisions would be made based on fact, not assumptions? The answer: defensible information on the value of their products and services to the organization.

To this end, we interviewed *funders* from the executive team about security issues and services; many in fact were impressed that one of their shared services groups was taking such a strategic approach. We also interviewed and administered a short questionnaire to peer leaders (*influencers*) regarding their security concerns and needs. Finally, we administered questionnaires to specific groups of product and service users—sales people at conventions where proprietary information could be stolen, distribution groups that worry about counterfeit drugs, employees whose roles required them to travel to risky countries at times, and so forth.

The data provided a rich texture for immediate decisions (see Figure 18.1).

- Some services such as travel security training were viewed as high value by Users, but not fully understood by *influencers*, who perhaps saw employees losing work time while at training. Communications about risks to the *influencers* cleared this up—and increased the attendance at the sessions.
- In contrast, sales representatives saw the security as over the top at off-site meetings and conferences. Few of the reps ever had a computer stolen or had lost critical sales decks. In response, security team members provided more reasons for their actions, so that they were not viewed as modern day James Bonds. When a computer was stolen at a conference the next year, the reps were much quicker to report the loss and to engage in the necessary actions to address the risks.
- Some *funders* were resistant to personal security details, again leading to a balance between the cloaking effect of some security actions and a commitment to greater self-vigilance actions by the executives.

In response to the ratings of various services, the CSO redistributed his resources, increasing efforts in some areas, improving processes such as investigations, and upgrading some resources such as IT security.

Determining how best to synthesize often requires the right analyses, which we will talk about next.

Synthesis of Information to
Knowledge within a Decision Framework

Once data have been gathered and analyzed (see Chapter 6) to convert data to information, we need to think about how this information feeds decisions. For example, recall the restaurant described earlier. Let's take a look at how information might affect decision making in the area of retention. The restaurant chain put a premium on the restaurant manager (RM). Turnover of these managers is highly disruptive, typically creating more turnover among employees in the restaurants. Also, previous analyses connecting the employee dashboard to customer dashboard information had shown that manager turnover often led to reduced customer visits per month and lower mystery shopper scores.[1] The organization wants to control manager turnover as much as possible while balancing the desires of some managers to be developed and promoted.

Information from surveys, performance information about the restaurant, and ratings by the area manager who oversees the RM can be integrated on a regular basis, perhaps quarterly, to create a "red flag" system that warns management of higher-risk locations for intervention. Periodic interviews by a third party can also provide additional in-depth information along with potential fixes. In this case, we would certainly want to use an index predictive of turnover from the strategic people survey, as described in Chapter 9, along with other data, to create a risk index that is calculated automatically so that we do not wait for a crisis to dig into—or worse yet, collect—data.

Another example comes from a global package delivery company. Executives had identified business outcomes they wanted to manage tightly: accidents, turnover and productivity of drivers, customer satisfaction, labor relations effectiveness, and several operating measures. Having made this decision, the company needed to consider what information would enable what decisions:

- Can we create an index that will predict labor relations risks?
- Can we obtain information that would help us prevent accidents?

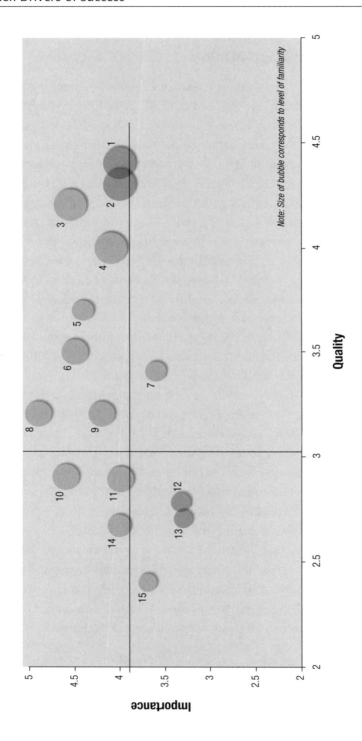

Note: Size of bubble corresponds to level of familiarity

Chart Value	Core Security Service	Quality	Importance	Familiarity
1	Special Event Security	4.40	4.00	4.40
2	Executive Protection	4.30	4.00	4.10
3	Access Control	4.20	4.55	4.00
4	Travel Security (awareness, training and services)	4.00	4.10	4.30
5	Security Awareness / Threat Management	3.70	4.40	3.00
6	Security Response	3.50	4.50	3.60
7	Consulting Advice (security solutions)	3.40	3.56	2.90
8	Information Protection	3.20	4.90	3.40
9	Physical Security Design	3.20	4.20	3.40
10	Crisis Management	2.90	4.60	3.40
11	Protection of patients, brand and product IP	2.89	4.00	3.67
12	Security Regulatory Compliance	2.78	3.33	2.70
13	Interface with Law Enforcement (local, federal, FDA, OCI)	2.70	3.30	2.60
14	Investigations	2.67	4.00	3.20
15	Intelligence & Risk Analysis	2.40	3.70	2.50

Figure 18.1 Funder's Ratings of Core Services

- How can we increase driver productivity?
- How can we increase speed of delivery?
- What information would help us predict turnover risks?
- How can we increase customer satisfaction without sacrificing productivity?

Given these objectives, we were able to build one omnibus employee survey that created predictive indices in each of these areas with bottom-line decisions already in mind, linked to the above questions. Information from employees (notably vehicle drivers) was then combined with information from the customer dashboard to identify locations that obtained both high customer satisfaction and high productivity. The characteristics of these locations were contrasted with ones that were low on customer satisfaction or productivity, yielding information about the characteristics that differentiate the desired drivers and locations from others. This data enabled the company to initiate communication, education, and process initiatives to bring more locations toward their target.

Putting It All Together

Table 18.2 shows how strategic thinking and the use of an employee dashboard can provide a master template for data collection, synthesis, and decisions. If you are working with a third-party vendor for survey or other data collection, this is a perfect opportunity to involve your consultant strategically in information planning. Another benefit of creating a master template is leveraging costs by putting together the most cost-effective design across a variety of information needs. *Every time you tackle an issue separately without integrated thinking and design, it costs you far more and is likely to cause more disruption in your organization.* In such situations, you are apt to receive comments such as, "We are always being surveyed about something, but it doesn't seem to make sense."

Below is a template for the organization of the future; some organizations are already well on their path to this. The issues being measured vary from spot measures to strategic long-term issues that

Table 18.2 Intelligence System Planner

Outcomes Desired	Information needed	Source
High retention of employees in pivotal jobs	Employee retention data	Employee database
High customer retention	Customer retention data	Customer database
Productivity	Route speed versus expected	Operations Report 5
Few accidents	Accident and safety info	Mo. Safety Report
Positive labor-relations climate	Contract ratification	Contract votes (region)
Brand and image	Customer reputation	Michigan Satisfaction Benchmarks
Leading Indicators		
Retention intentions	Retention index	ACE survey
Employee engagement	Engagement index	ACE survey
Employee alignment	Alignment index	ACE survey
Labor-relations attitudes & drivers	Labor index	ACE survey
Safety attitudes, behaviors	Safety index	ACE survey; behavioral assessment
Service competencies/attitudes	Capabilities index	ACE survey; supervisory review
Customer affinity	Mirror index*	ACE survey; customer complaints
Supervisor effectiveness	Supervisor index	ACE survey; 360
Chairman credibility	Top L. index	ACE survey; spot speech polls

*Mirroring is a method for understanding employee-customer affinity—how well the employee understands and can accurately report on customer views; index is created by comparing employee and customer information on common dimensions.

change slowly. This organization has carved out a master plan for its survey use that addresses the end goals of productivity, retention for "A" jobs, customer loyalty, and internal value in the supply chain. From those goals, executives in the company identified the measures to capture those outcomes, along with a host of drivers of those outcomes.

Timing

The last issue we wish to address regarding employee information systems is timing. A key to timely and relevant information is having various databases loaded and ready to go for any contingency, whether it be a single incident such as a poll of the chairman's latest speech (see Table 18.2) or an urgent need to survey the West Coast sales organization.

Programmatic Assessments

At one end of the spectrum is a full strategic survey, such as ACE, administered on a regular interval, perhaps annually or semiannually. This type of survey is intended to connect with a variety of decisions needed in organizations as well as to track high-level indices that may be on the organization's scorecard. These types of surveys or assessments provide the following benefits:

- Pinpointed information about how well the strategy is being executed
- General organizational health indices (for example, labor relations, safety, diversity)
- Leading indicators (such as ACE) of important business outcomes (for example, productivity, customer loyalty)
- Identification of employee and operational gaps
- Topical issues that are being piggybacked on this more strategic tool

The last two items are only capturing information relevant to that time period, which is useful in the case of topical issues that have a fleeting time relevancy. Programmatic assessments are a good vehicle for identifying issues that have a longer time span (for example, growing ethical concerns or labor relations declines).

Planned Assessments

Pulse surveys and other more frequent assessments can be invaluable in handling a number of issues:

- Assessing progress during periods of change (such as a merger or transformation). We have often used frequent—as short a biweekly in the first stages of merger—surveys and focus groups to identify rumors, avert problems, and test integration during this fragile period.

- Assessing progress on action implementation in areas targeted for change, some perhaps the result of a more programmatic survey (such as ACE) and its subsequent prioritization of issues.

- Digging deeper into issues that may have been flagged because of missed targets, perhaps for a critical scorecard measure, or other information that suggests a deeper investigation is warranted. For example, if a high-level ethics index on the broad ACE survey comes back low in five units, then a more robust survey of ethical issues along with focus groups and interviews is likely warranted. Increasing safety problems or lost-time accidents might indicate that a particular plant needs to conduct a full safety survey instead of a short index.

- Exploring topical issues. One client rolled out a new retail concept in two major markets, and we used surveys to obtain timely information from retail locations in those markets; waiting for regular programmatic surveys would have been of little value.

Tactical Spot Assessments

There are times when planning data collection is not practical; the organization must simply be ready:

- Short-term information. Polls, shown, for example, in Table 18.2, can be helpful in understanding brand and reputation. This organization found that the reactions to the chairman's speeches, because of the large size of the organization and its public nature, was a reliable index of public reaction (public polls were also taken periodically) and was helpful in gauging the credibility of senior leadership—a predictor of many crucial outcomes.

- Process problems. When quality is at stake, such as a product malfunction or tampering, quick surveys can be helpful to find out how the organization or the public is faring. During such crises or periods of stress, employee engagement, leader credibility, trust, and other dimensions can be at risk. Better to know than to guess.

Though these two chapters on intelligence systems are not intended to cover all the many operational issues related to their successful execution, we hope they will provide a template for thinking about how your organization plans, organizes, and deploys measures in a more integrated and effective manner.

Action Tips

1. If you performed an audit as described in the Chapter 17's Action Tips, take a closer look at the employee or labor-related measures. How many are gathered via surveys? Are there opportunities to integrate or to combine those into fewer data collection vehicles?
2. Take a look at the intelligence system planner in Table 18.2. Construct one that is right for your organization.
   a. Do you have programmatic, planned, and tactical approaches, as we described in this chapter?
   b. Have you incorporated design, analysis, and synthesis into the planning?
   a. Have you designed the measures with the decision in mind?
      i. Have you analyzed information into indices that will be more reliable and provide richer understanding and a better decision?
      ii. Do you perform regular analyses, integrating information across multiple data sets that will provide a more comprehensive answer to important questions?
      iii. Do you have both leading and lagging indicators?

Chapter 19

Mass Customizing Your Workforce: Using Measurement to Optimize Your Talent

"Millennials will not limit diversity to just race, ethnicity, or even sex anymore. They will also define diversity by thinking style, educational background, geographic location, generation, avocation, lifestyle, sexual orientation, work experience, and more."[1]

—Lancaster and Stillman, 2002

"Don't assume you know all about me."

—A Millennial, a Generation X member, and a Baby Boomer

We live in a dramatically changing world in terms of information. Only a few decades ago, information was tough to obtain, often flawed, and costly. Today, information is ubiquitous, cheap, and at times overwhelming. This reality poses unique challenges to organizations. How can you sort out the informational wheat from the chaff? In Chapter 2 we discussed how you can narrow down your field of inquiry to those areas that are most strategic to your organization. Why ask about innovation if your organization does not value it? Why focus on employee benefits in your inquiries if you are not prepared to tackle any changes? Why add lots of questions on speed to market if you are in a mature market that is not competing on speed? We learned that we can hone topics and questions in our surveys, interviews, or focus groups to items that particularly matter to our organization's individual strategy or focus.

In Chapter 6, we learned that presenting all the information we possess to the leadership team or other key stakeholders does not make sense, especially if we want these busy people to focus on the most demanding issues. We learned that we can also slice the data to provide richer information to these stakeholders. Do longer-tenure employees feel the same about an issue as newcomers? Do high performers view workload or pay for performance differently from lower performers? Do majority and minority employees feel differently about promotional opportunities?

We also discussed the importance of narrowing the focus of action, perhaps only targeting groups for which the data are relevant, such as for low-scoring leaders. Strategic choices involve making decisions about what is going to be most and least relevant in a particular situation. Some groups will need a great deal of information whereas others may need narrower information slices.

We also know that *data*, *information*, and *knowledge* are three different levels of value creation. Data may include observations or facts or opinions. Information codifies those data into understandable groupings or patterns. Knowledge, however, requires taking information and making it contextually relevant and rich to yourself and to others. What do I need to know to make a good decision? What are the norms of what others are able to do in my situation? What are the probabilities of success or failure if I act on this information? Will this information help others learn to take or avoid actions that have critical outcomes?

We believe a main goal is to move from data that are now plentiful, cheap, and intimidating to knowledge that is particularly relevant to an individual, group, or organization. Even information that is well codified and packaged but that lies dormant is of little use and is an unaffordable luxury in the new marketplace. We must become ever better at transforming this information into knowledge that can be shared, compared, and valued for its ability to instruct our decision making.

This chapter will address how we can do a better job of codifying data in ways that enable our organization to optimize its talent—the collective experiences, skills, knowledge, and abilities of its workforce or other forms of labor. We will address the issue of segmentation, in particular looking at employees as a group for which a better understanding of different needs, expectations, and performance drivers can greatly enhance knowledge and decisions.

Fair or Equal?

Organizations—particularly in Europe and North America—have moved through an era of focusing on equal or the same treatment of diverse peoples, often in the interest of fair treatment. But has it been fair?

Many parts of society, including work organizations, have often failed to acknowledge, respect, or leverage appropriate differences in needs, experiences, personal values, and preferred styles of working. Being *fair* rather than *equal* may be more consequential to optimizing talent in the future. Most organizations have yet to take major strides to mass-customize[2] programs, policies, initiatives, developmental needs, competencies, and desires of these different segments of the workforce.

Early attempts at mass customization in the 1980s focused on employee benefits, with the introduction of flexible benefits plans. The overall goal was cost containment and employee satisfaction in an era of benefits entitlements, realizing that if some people did not need or value certain benefits, why not put those costs to better uses? To that end, many companies implemented "cafeteria" plans with greater flexibility in what employees could choose but with caps on overall costs. Although this movement seemed to make a lot of sense, this way of thinking was not often extended to other areas of the workplace. For example, most firms still had rigid policies about work hours, work location, development steps, career ladders, and so forth. Today there is growing realization not only that individuals are truly unique, requiring flexible policies and organizational features, but that uniqueness can be leveraged for higher performance, assuming the organization manages it correctly. An individual is not simply young, male, short-tenured, and Asian, but instead he will have a distinct profile of interests, competencies, career goals, and family needs that will influence how much he contributes to the organization and vice versa.

Intuitively, we know that people have individual differences, but we often take the psychologically and economically easier cost-benefit route of classifying people in larger clusters. Psychologically and physiologically our brains are wired to want to classify people to make it easier to navigate our lives. We more easily think of categories in which people can be quickly classified—"Oh, he is the athlete, which means . . . ," or "She is very attractive, which means . . . " You fill in the bias—we have plenty of them! In recent years, profiling has been a major dilemma for police departments and other groups. In profiling, someone or a group—for example, a police department—takes either stereotypical views of a group or uses statistical data on crimes that occur with the group or in the neighborhood and generalizes them to all members of that group. The individuals who do not fit that profile are unduly classified and treated inappropriately for whom they really are.

Such treatment occurs in many everyday activities. Do you assume that a young unmarried employee does not need family time to balance work demands? Do you assume that a 48-year-old employee might not want to move to part time or to retire early, only to find that person leaving the organization earlier than you desired? Do you assume that a young female recently married is likely to be out with children in a few months or years and would probably not want an assignment that would require her to move abroad? Do you assume that a high performer will also be a good leader of others?

Though we will never eliminate generalizations completely, companies incur organizational (and personal) costs of not employing better decision models to help optimize talent and workforce investments. Most of us now realize that by stereotyping protected classes of people—minorities, woman, older adults, for example—we have missed many opportunities. However, there is far greater opportunity for both the organization and the employees in understanding individuals as clusters of many other groupings: needs, values, experiences, work preferences, competencies, and so forth. Consider the following scenarios:

- What if we have one cluster of highly talented individuals who have transient work needs? Do we have a strategy for extracting value from this cluster?
- Do we have effective processes for addressing individuals who are superb technically but perhaps not great at managing people? How do they advance in the organization? Might they not contribute more value in a technical role than as a mediocre manager?
- Do we have effective policies to handle an employee who has an immense desire to increase her education and finds a class at the local college that runs from 10:00 a.m. to noon three days a week? If she is willing to work extra hours to make up for this time, can we accommodate her request?

These are a few of the questions that represent the challenges and opportunities facing organizations today. And as you will see, measurement plays a major role.

Why Bother?

You might ask, why bother? At the time of this writing, the global economy has been slumping. Hiring managers should have their pick of employees. Interestingly enough, that model only works when supply and demand are incredibly out of balance, as in periods of high unemployment and surplus skills. However, despite the high unemployment in recent years, in almost every talent interview conducted by the authors, leaders discussed skills shortages. Many described difficulties in finding sufficient talent in a variety of skill groups: engineering and scientific jobs, specialty nurses, middle managers, skilled trades such as electricians or welders, and many others. In fact, a nuclear power plant in the United States reported having to delay construction of its new power plant until it could train welders because it could not find enough skilled workers.

Some younger workers are unwilling to take jobs they do not like or that have unappealing work features such as working as independently rather than with a team.[3] Perhaps the firm is perceived to lack green values or has been involved in public scandals or lacks volunteerism opportunities. In the recent recession, many people have opted to go back to school rather than take an onerous job. Or they may take several part-time roles that are expected to be transient until they find a better fit.

Even if you could "force" people to work because of the economics, is that what you really want? People who have low Engagement can hurt organizations more than help. They may be there physically, but not mentally. Their hearts are not in it. Their lackluster attitude means the employer is not getting the best effort. Also, they may not be aligned with the mission and values. If you are a retailer, they may hate your brand and type of clothing, but "it's a job!" What image does that project to the customer? And as the economy improves, all of those people are likely to bolt, leaving you looking for people who really fit—a big cost!

If you work for a global organization, it probably already has pockets of economic growth around the globe. The challenge for you is finding people who fit—who are Aligned, Capable, and Engaged in your organization's mission. The ACE model provides a window for thinking about how we better manage variation in our labor pool and workforce. In many ways, if someone is Aligned, Capable, and Engaged, his or her other differences do not matter. The challenge is finding people who are high ACE, regardless of stereotypes about a particular class they belong to.

Segmentation Heaven

Of late, many organizations have thought about the subject of managing at an individual level. Although this is the right kind of thinking, measuring and managing at this level can be a challenge. We applaud organizations that are building management skills that enable leaders to do a better job of having the insight and skills to assess their employees' differences and to balance individual needs with organization goals. This is as much art as science because supervisors do not always have a match between their resources and business needs.

Other levels encounter this situation as well. One of the authors (Schiemann) served on a board of directors that constantly faced this challenge. With only 12 board members, selecting and then balancing board member capabilities and interests with the required roles of the board was difficult. Furthermore, the needs of the board were also changing over time. In this case, the board needed more market and brand expertise as well as stronger connections to top leaders, but the need to balance academic and practitioner members at times limited the ability to find the right mix of skills at the right time. It required thinking about alternative structures such as creating an outside fund-raising advisory group that leveraged the limited skills represented on the board.

How Can Surveys and Other Measures Help?

Typically, surveys are analyzed by major demographic groups. However, with increasing connectivity to other databases, more powerful analyses are possible.[4] For example, we can increasingly make comparisons of groups such as high vs. low performers. Organizations are already making many other types of comparisons: high- vs. low-potential employees, levels of volunteerism, benefits clusters, interest groups, participation in corporate programs, skills, and so forth.

Almost anything in an employee database, if properly guarded for anonymity, might provide decision value. What if your high-potential employees as a group began to show declining scores on a predictive index of turnover? Knowing this information would enable you to target this group to identify causes and to take corrective action. Or what if certain job groups with specific educational or skills levels showed a propensity to be union prone? Such information would allow the organization to discern why the group scores lower on a labor relations predictor index and to take appropriate actions relative to the organization's labor goals.

Another major opportunity is afforded in leader development. Classifying leaders by the eight ACE profiles (refer to Table 4.1 in Chapter 4) of employees they manage lets the organization provide targeted resources to improve these leaders. For some, training might be called for, for others coaching. And yet, those with low Alignment scores might need help with business acumen or performance management.

Digging Deeper

However, we could also take our analyses a step further. What if we could better capture information on employees in a large team or division, enabling us to understand the mix of different individual characteristics across needs, experiences, competencies, and so forth?

- Are there clusters of common need types? Do we have a balance of people whose needs are complementary, such as preferred working hours? For example, in a call center, is there a mix of employees that would allow us to staff weekly schedules while matching personal demands on many of the employees?
- Are there clusters of common complementary experiences? If we are investing in partnerships with India, do we have sufficient skills or cultural understanding among some clusters of talent to transfer to other clusters? If everyone is a pro with Microsoft software, what happens if the organization needs to interface with Apple, Droid, or Linux software?

When she was with the Concours Group, Tamara Erickson took another approach. She reported research that identified employee typologies of different predictable characteristics, such as dominance of transient workers, high achievers, or those who are comfortable but not willing to push the envelope, and so forth.[5] These groupings, if discovered, could help in tailoring advancement, training, benefits, mentoring, and work experiences. That is, by better understanding need profiles, an organization can more effectively allocate its scarce resources in ways that create improved fit.

Another example is affinity groups, increasingly prolific as the boundaries between corporate and personal lives recede. Frequent travelers, for example, may find benefits in being members of particular interest groups (for example, scuba, sailing, bird watching). This involvement might afford better work/life integration, combining business travel with personal vacationing. Volunteer groups from the same company might build stronger bonds across different functional groups that were once silos.

Privacy issues withstanding, an organization could easily integrate databases from employee surveys, HRIS databases, and Internet groups such as LinkedIn or Facebook to create a richer information pool to help executives and their employees make wiser decisions. Organizations such as IBM or Accenture already have large competency, experience, and interest banks that allow them to quickly figure out how they might staff a new team in Shanghai or Sydney or to replace exiting members of a team.

Generational Differences?

You may have noticed we have said little about segmenting on generational differences. In fact, many common experiences are shared by members of certain generations, such as the access and expertise of Millennials in computer technology, gaming, and the Internet. Many Baby Boomers feel handicapped, and many, in fact, rely on their children to keep them "in the technology game." These cohorts also have different habits, often shaped by technology, economic periods, or other cultural issues. For example, Millennials feel far more comfortable in a global world; they have been exposed to global events their entire life. Some evidence also suggests that they are more team focused, even dependent.

The popular press is filled with articles describing specific differences between the generations, but many of these assertions have little scientific support. If you think about it, grouping all adults into five generational buckets and generalizing about them is not much different from stereotyping on ethnicity or gender! Some Boomers work part time; some members of Generation X work long hours; and some Millennials care more about salary than about development. As Tamara Erickson noted, generations, such as Baby Boomers, often project their own values on to other generations.[6] For example, she argued that the "trophy Y-generation," always needing to get an award for something, was driven more by their Baby Boomer parents' needs for achievement, perhaps a reflection of the level of competition during the overwhelming crush of the baby boom.

Jennifer Deal at the Center for Creative Leadership has reported in her research that many of the common characteristics purported to be uniquely generational can be attributed to one's life stage.[7] Many Baby Boomers or members of Generation X were idealistic, wanting to change the world when they were in their late teens or twenties. Each group was savvy with the technology of the times. And each group was a product of social issues prevalent during those periods, from extreme racial strife during the Baby Boom and the threat of nuclear war during the Cold War. For younger generations today, issues such as identity theft, immigration, or pandemics are constantly at play.

Generations are a lazy way to think about differences. There is an assumption that each generation is homogenous. But does a Boomer who served in Vietnam necessarily have the same values and motivations as one who refused to serve? Is a Millennial who grew up in rural poverty the same as one from a wealthy suburb? The idea of generations grew out of the belief that a cohort with shared developmental and life experiences will have similarities in behaviors, interests, and attitudes. Yet we cannot assume that two people of similar age have had similar formative experiences any more than we can assume two people of color will have led similar lives. Generational stereotypes are easy because we can all come up with anecdotal examples to support them. Remember that the plural of anecdote is not "data."

Generational classification is too blunt a tool to be depended on for the breadth in characteristics that exist today. Clusters or segments based on actual needs, interests, and skills are far more meaningful and actionable.

Dominic Orr, president of Aruba Networks, a wireless networking firm, argues that all people work for three things: impact, fun, and rewards.[8] How they view those three may be different because of their backgrounds, experiences, life stage, and so forth. CEO Phil Libin of Evernote[9] focuses instead on changes in the environment *today* that may help all employees be more productive, such as getting rid of vacations. He said in an interview, "They can take as much time as they want, as long as they get their job done. Frankly, we want to treat employees like adults, and we don't want being in the office to seem like a punishment."[10]

Your Measures May Also Influence How You Segment

Most organizations, and many researchers, still administer their surveys primarily with five-point scale items such as, "I like working here," rated from *strongly agree* to *strongly disagree*. But other types of questions and scales can provide different ways to potentially group individuals. Although a positive affective feeling such as satisfaction with something is helpful, other aspects may play a part. In Chapter 3 on internal value assessment, for example, we discussed importance and awareness ratings in addition to ratings of performance. Someone might rate your function (or a product or service of your function) high or low in performance, but you may discount or put a premium on this rating based on the rater's level of awareness or how important he or she rates this deliverable. Context is key. Such classifications allow a manager to focus on both those who are knowledgeable (aware) and those who see the service as important.

Researchers such as Karen Stephenson have demonstrated that rich network information can be garnered by asking about frequency of contact on critical dimensions, such as: Who do you go to for expert knowledge? Who do you go to for social contact? Who do you interact with on critical decisions? Her network analyses allow an organization to classify individuals—not clusters of employees—in terms of leadership potential, their role as gatekeepers or information hubs, their level of influence, and so forth.

N=1

As privacy laws change and individuals' comfort with sharing more information increases, additional opportunities may exist to make better use of a broader set of data sources to optimize talent.

A cutting-edge area is exploring individual feedback. We can actually look at the ACE scores of individuals and provide feedback on their profile that will help them think about their Alignment, Capabilities, and Engagement. This information is a powerful self-development or career decision tool:

- Those with low Alignment scores could use this feedback for conversations with their supervisor regarding additional information that is needed, conflicts with other teams, or concerns about the direction of the company.
- Employees reporting low Capability scores might discuss teamwork issues with their team leader or person-job fit with human resources or innovation concerns with a research council. Perhaps these individuals are not getting the information or resources they need to optimize their performance.
- Low Engagement individuals can take additional actions to help them become highly engaged or to decide to leave:
  - Talk to human resources or other ombudsmen in the organization about supervisory issues, such as demeaning communication or fairness issues, whatever is the root cause of their low Engagement
  - Talk to their manager about growth concerns, if they are inhibiting high Engagement
  - Submit recommendations to secure hotlines or suggestion vehicles regarding poor recognition, if that is the core engagement issue
  - Decide to leave—it might be better to help coach low Engagement individuals to head for greener pastures. This type of guidance would be analogous to employees receiving an interest inventory telling them that an engineering or teaching role might not be a good fit for their temperament, information that helps them take another path.

Although current laws on how much information can be shared vary by country, if done in a trusting and supportive environment, this kind of information sharing could enable individuals to pinpoint areas where they are not operating at an optimal level. The analogy is perhaps high school or private counselors. Counselors can use individual test scores, grades, interest inventories, and style interviews to recommend the right college that might fit a particular student. Some take this advice to heart more than others.

In the workplace, though this information may not be acted on by all individuals, many may relish the opportunity to grow and increase their value, especially in an emerging environment in which personal as well as organizational value will be paramount for survival. For example, one way to share information is for the vendor managing the data to confidentially send ACE scores or other relevant indices to the employee, along with recommendations for how each employee can use that information. Communications would be required at the beginning of the survey process, informing survey participants that individual information would be shared in this way. For example, someone with high Alignment and Engagement but low Capabilities could receive guidance regarding the courses of action others had taken to enhance their Capabilities. Areas such as skills-job fit, communications, or teamwork would be potential realms of focus.

This approach will obviously require different communications, assurances, and training by individuals about how they can navigate their own value and optimize trade-offs between the organization and their careers.

This nascent area still needs development, but organizations can take a host of actions to use information more strategically than their competitors and to optimize their talent.

Action Tips

1. Consider how well your organization currently detects information regarding groups of individuals that might enable it to make more effective decisions:
    a. Do you currently know how low vs. high performers view key issues in the organization: staffing, innovation, communications, compensation?

b. Do you segment information by age, tenure, or other maturational classifications? Has that information helped you to tailor recruiting, communication, benefits, or retention policies?

c. Do you identify need clusters such as work hours and styles, high- vs. low-growth needs?

d. Do you identify groups such as high- vs. low-potential leaders? Have you validated those groupings? Do they help optimize your selection and development of leaders?

e. Visit library.metrus.com for a list of additional questions and a checklist of potential opportunities

VIII

A CALL TO ACTION

Throughout the book we have described the development of strategic intelligence systems, beginning with the development of a strategy map, then discussed key strategic indicators, and continued on to an assessment of each component of the measurement system.

In this section we provide an inventory you can use to assess the state of your organization's strategic intelligence systems and to begin to construct a road map for improvement. A link is also provided to an in-depth online version of the inventory.

Because the management of your strategic intelligence systems is as important as the quality of the measures it includes, we also provide recommendations for maximizing the effectiveness of your organization's intelligence systems.

Chapter 20

Building Your Strategic Intelligence System

An integrated strategic intelligence system using the measurement tools discussed throughout this book is a cornerstone of effective strategy implementation. As noted in Chapter 17, fragmented, one-issue-at-a-time attempts to address business challenges are more likely to be costly, disruptive, and ineffective than integrated approaches.

The components and the functioning of an integrated strategic intelligence system are described in depth in Chapters 17 and 18. Here, we offer an inventory that enables you to assess the current state of strategic intelligence in your organization and to identify the steps that you need to take to build an optimal strategic intelligence system (see Table 20.1). Consider the inventory as a call to action for your organization as you strive to build and sustain a competitive edge.

The inventory lists the components of a strategic intelligence system, asks you to rate the extent to which you agree or disagree that each statement describes your organization's current performance, and provides a space for you to indicate the next steps needed for improvement in your organization.

The more of these components you have up and running, the better off you are, but only if the system is well integrated, consisting of measures that are widely shared, valued, and used for improvement.

A more comprehensive version of the inventory is posted on the book website (library.metrus.com). You can complete the full version to drill down further on the issues covered in the inventory that appears here.

Table 20.1 Strategic Intelligence Inventory

Strategic intelligence component	Strongly Agree (5) Strongly Disagree (1)	Next action step to improve
1. You can infer our business strategy from our strategic measures.	5 4 3 2 1	
2. We have a scorecard with 20 or fewer measures for the organization as a whole.	5 4 3 2 1	
3. We have a talent scorecard or clearly defined talent measures.	5 4 3 2 1	
4. There is an ongoing measurement program that tracks the value that internal departments provide to each other.	5 4 3 2 1	
5. We conduct employee surveys at least annually.	5 4 3 2 1	
6. The senior team buys into and uses the findings from our strategic employee survey to make important decisions.	5 4 3 2 1	
7. We have specific questions on the survey that measure unique elements of our business strategy.	5 4 3 2 1	
8. We use analytics to link employee survey findings to business outcomes such as employee retention and turnover, customer satisfaction and value, and financial performance.	5 4 3 2 1	
9. We hold managers accountable for improvements in survey score results in areas that were targeted for action and improvement.	5 4 3 2 1	
10. We use pulse surveys of employees several times each year (for example, to track progress on priority survey issues or to assess reactions to communications or initiatives).	5 4 3 2 1	
11. We have good measures of the effectiveness of our recruiting and hiring process.	5 4 3 2 1	
12. We have good measures of our effectiveness in acculturating employees in the organization.	5 4 3 2 1	
13. Our employee survey has indicators that help us understand turnover threats.	5 4 3 2 1	
14. We have ongoing measures in place that tell us how well managers optimize the talent that they lead or coach.	5 4 3 2 1	
15. We have measures of senior leadership's effectiveness in communicating and guiding organizational performance.	5 4 3 2 1	
16. We have ongoing measures of our employees' views of the extent to which we live by our core values.	5 4 3 2 1	

17. Senior management actively uses measures of values to take action when scores are unfavorable.	5 4 3 2 1	
18. Our organization has an integrated system to obtain, store, and deliver information from employees to the right decision makers at the right time.	5 4 3 2 1	
19. Strategic measures are reviewed frequently, with action plans put in place to close gaps.	5 4 3 2 1	
20. Our organization is effective at mining and leveraging information to arrive at new insights and conclusions about organizational performance or talent management.	5 4 3 2 1	

Add up your scores. A perfect score is 100.
- If you score 86 or higher, consider your measurement system to be among the best.
- Scores between 75-85 are doing well but have some key areas that could be enhanced to optimize talent and to improve organizational performance.
- Scores between 60-74 have some pockets of strengths but definitely need enhancements in other areas to stay competitive.
- Scores below 60 indicate serious concerns about the ability to leverage information to stay competitive.

As we noted at the beginning of the book, employees are a great source of information about your organization. Gathering, analyzing, and deploying information from your employees to make business decisions is a leading element of effective management.

As you move forward to develop an integrated strategic intelligence system, remember the following recommendations for maximizing its effectiveness as a management tool:

1. Diagnose before you prescribe solutions; base actions on facts and evidence.
2. Always, always, always think about your strategy, your vision, and your mission before you decide what to measure.
3. Create, communicate, and use values or guiding principles to shape behaviors and guide decisions. They must be lived by top people, measured, and then reinforced over time.
4. Coordinate strategic measures—for example, do people we hire create high impact?—but also effectiveness measures—for example, do people we hire stay?—and transactional/efficiency measures—for example, what is our average time to hire? The

best organizations have all three levels; most miss the strategic ones and too often lead with the tactical.

5. Work to unleash the power of your employee survey. Most organizations can get far more survey return on investment than they do today.

6. Employee surveys can and should be linked to the talent lifecycle. We must manage the lifecycle, but we need measures that are well interconnected to optimize talent management.

7. Think about using strategic measures to move from talent management to talent optimization—this is where the ACE framework comes in!

8. Put surveys to work on your internal and external supply chain, including functions such as IT, Human Resources, Marketing, R&D, and Finance. These functions, along with external providers, should be assessed for ways to increase value that when improved will help overall organizational performance.

9. Begin building strong intelligence systems to manage all the information you need to make sound business decisions—and to anticipate future trends and issues.

10. Remember that ongoing communication of survey results and actions based on the results is critical for the effectiveness of a strategic intelligence system. Survey measurement is a type of structured dialogue with employees that has the greatest impact if it is ongoing and actively managed.

Good luck, and remember the information tools supporting this book:

- library.metrus.com
- www.metrus.com
- Metrus hotline: 908-231-1900 or info@metrus.com

If the information posted does not help, please contact us to see if we can answer your questions.

Endnotes

In the course of preparing this book, the Metrus Institute, the research and analysis division of Metrus Group, Inc., conducted approximately 100 interviews with senior leaders regarding talent and business issues. Individuals and content referenced but not directly cited in the text are based on these interviews. We thank these leaders for their candor and willingness to support our research.

Chapter 2

1. Adam Bryant, "A Simple Plan: Three Goals for Everyone," *New York Times*, November 14, 2010, http://www.nytimes.com/2010/11/14/business/14corner.html?pagewanted= all.
2. William A. Schiemann and John H. Lingle, *Bullseye!: Hitting Your Strategic Targets Through High-Impact Measurement* (New York: Free Press, 1999).
3. The model shown here is a representative view of an actual map, but it has been adapted both to protect confidential information and to highlight points being made in this book. Some concepts shown in earlier publications are omitted here, and a few have been added. There are some variations in naming the concepts to make them more accessible to today's reader.

Chapter 3

1. Jerry H. Seibert and William A. Schiemann, "Reversing Course: Survey Sheds Light on Pitfalls of Outsourcing," *Quality Progress*, July 2011, 37-43.
2. Alfred Torres, "Recruitment Process Outsourcing," Executive Session on Managing Talent: Optimizing Global Talent Acquisition, June 22, 2011, Basking Ridge, NJ.
3. Jerry H. Seibert and John Lingle, "Internal Customer Service: Has It Improved?," *Quality Progress*, March 2007, 35-40.
4. Ibid.

Chapter 4

1. William A. Schiemann, "People Equity: A New Paradigm for Measuring and Managing Human Capital," *Human Resource Planning* 29, no. 1 (2006).
2. Jerry H. Seibert and John Lingle, "Internal Customer Service: Has It Improved?," *Quality Progress*, March 2007, 35-40; Jerry H. Seibert and William A. Schiemann, "Power to the People," *Quality Progress*, April 2010, 24-30.
3. This is a partial view of the organization; not all countries or groups are included in this chart.
4. These data represent one company and are not indicative of the general results of these countries or regions.
5. William A. Schiemann, "Organizational Change: Lessons from a Turnaround," *Management Review* 81, no. 4 (1992): 34-37.

Chapter 6

1. Daniel H. Pink, *A Whole New Mind: Why Right-Brainers Will Rule the Future*, (New York: Penguin, 2005).
2. For example, relative weights analysis (RWA) is a recent refinement of regression analysis that is ideal for survey data. It produces more robust predictive models because it effectively takes into account the many interrelationships (correlations) among

the issues addressed in an employee survey. For a useful summary of RWA, see Kyle M. Lundby and Jeff J. Johnson, "Relative Weights of Predictors: What Is Important When Many Forces Are Operating," in *Getting Action from Organizational Surveys: New Concepts, Technologies and Applications* (San Francisco: Jossey-Bass, 2006), 326-351.

Chapter 7

1. Brian S. Morgan and William A. Schiemann, "Measuring People and Performance: Closing the Gaps," *Quality Progress*, January 1999, 47-53.

Chapter 8

1. Adam Bryant, "Tearing Down All the Silos in a Company," *New York Times*, February 13, 2011, http://www.nytimes.com/2011/02/13/business/13corner.html.
2. Adam Bryant, "In One Adjective, Please Tell Me Who You Are," *New York Times*, May 20, 2012, http://www.nytimes.com/2012/05/20/business/chris-barbin-of-appirio-on-boiling-down-answers.html.
3. Ibid.
4. Karl Ahlrichs, "Uncommon Knowledge: Align Your Strategy with Applicant Values Before They're Hired," (presentation, Society for Human Resource Management, Strategy Conference, Palm Springs, CA, October 12, 2007).
5. Adam Bryant, "Tearing Down All the Silos in a Company," 2011.

Chapter 9

1. Joe Light, "Exiting Workers Are More Disgruntled," *Wall Street Journal*, August 8, 2011.
2. Mark A. Huselid, Brian E. Becker, and Richard W. Beatty, *The Workforce Scorecard: Managing Human Capital to Execute Strategy* (Boston: Harvard Business School Press, 2005), 84-89.

3. John W. Boudreau, *Retooling HR: Using Proven Business Tools to Make Better Decisions About Talent* (Boston: Harvard Business Press, 2010).

4. John W. Boudreau and Peter M. Ramstad, *Beyond HR: The New Science of Human Capital* (Boston: Harvard Business School Press, 2007).

5. Karen Stephenson, "Trafficking in Trust: The Art and Science of Human Knowledge Networks," in *Enlightened Power: How Women Are Transforming Practice and Leadership* (San Francisco: Jossey Bass, 2005), 243-265; Karen Stephenson and M. Zelen, "Rethinking Centrality: Methods and Examples," *Social Networks* 11 (1999): 1-39; Karen Stephenson, "From Tiananmen to Tahrir: Knowing One's Place in the 21st Century," *Organizational Dynamics* 40 (2011): 281-291.

6. These ratios may be affected by strong or weak job markets. It is more important to arrive at a ratio based on a market in which job switching is realistic because that is the market that is most risky for organizational loss.

7. Wayne Cascio and John W. Boudreau, *Investing in People: Financial Impact of Human Resource Initiatives* (Upper Saddle River, NJ: FT Press, 2008), 67-98; William A. Schiemann, *Reinventing Talent Management: How to Maximize Performance in the New Marketplace* (Hoboken, NJ: John Wiley; Alexandria, VA: Society for Human Resource Management, 2009), 219-235.

8. William A. Schiemann, *The ACE Advantage: How Smart Companies Unleash Talent for Optimal Performance* (Alexandria, VA: Society for Human Resource Management, 2012), 24.

9. Joe Light, "Exiting Workers Are More Disgruntled," *Wall Street Journal*, August 8, 2011.

10. Ibid.

11. Accenture Alumni Network, 2012, https://www.accenture alumni.com.

12. Deloitte's alumni newsletter, *The Network*, August 2011, http://www.deloitte.com/assets/Dcom-UnitedStates/Local%20Assets/Documents/Alumni/us_alumni_the_network%20aug_2011_10182011.pdf.

Chapter 10

1. David V. Day, *Developing Leadership Talent: A Guide to Succession Planning and Leadership Development*, SHRM Foundation's Effective Practice Guidelines Series (Alexandria, VA: SHRM Foundation, 2007).

2. William A. Schiemann, *The ACE Advantage: How Smart Companies Unleash Talent for Optimal Performance* (Alexandria, VA: Society for Human Resource Management, 2012).

3. Adam Bryant, "C.E.O. or Not, You Always Need Feedback," *New York Times*, May 13, 2012, http://www.nytimes.com/2012/05/13/business/deborah-farrington-of-starvest-on-evaluating-ceos.html.

Chapter 11

1. Wal-Mart, "Basic Beliefs and Values," http://ethics.walmartstores.com/StatementOfEthics/BasicBeliefs.aspx, June 2012.

2. Google, "Ten Things We Know to Be True," http://www.google.com/about/company/philosophy/.

3. David Barstow, "Vast Mexico Bribery Case Hushed Up by Wal-Mart after Top-Level Struggle," *New York Times*, April 22, 2012, http://www.nytimes.com/2012/04/22/business/at-wal-mart-in-mexico-a-bribe-inquiry-silenced.html?pagewanted=all.

4. The Ritz-Carlton website, "Gold Standards," 2012, http://corporate.ritzcarlton.com/en/about/goldstandards.htm.

5. WD-40 Company, "About WD-40Company: WD-40 Company Values and Mission," 2012, http://www.wd40company.com/about/values/.

6. Geoff in Corporate, "Google: Ten Things We Know to Be True," *Manifesto Project* (blog), March 14, 2011, http://www.1000manifestos.com/google-ten-things-know-be-true/.

7. U.S. Chemical Safety and Hazard Investigation Board, *Investigation Report: Refinery Explosion and Fire; BP: Texas City, Texas, March 23, 2005*, Report No. 2005-04-I-TX (Washington, DC: U.S. Chemical Safety and Hazard Investigation Board, 2007), 26.

8. Dan Kurzman, *A Killing Wind: Inside Union Carbide and the Bhopal Catastrophe* (New York: McGraw-Hill, 1987).

9. DuPont, "Workplace Safety," 2012, http://www2.dupont.com/Sustainable_Solutions/en_GB/workplace_safety_management_11.htm.

10. Adam Bryant, "In One Adjective, Please Tell Me Who You Are," *New York Times*, May 20, 2012, http://www.nytimes.com/2012/05/20/business/chris-barbin-of-appirio-on-boiling-down-answers.html.

11. Adam Bryant, "Order is Great. It's Bureaucracy That's Stifling," *New York Times*, May 1, 2011, http://www.nytimes.com/2011/05/01/business/01corner.html?pagewanted=all.

Chapter 12

1. Labaton Sucharow LLP, *Wall Street, Fleet Street, Main Street: Corporate Integrity at a Crossroads; United States & United Kingdom Financial Services Industry Survey* (New York: Labaton Sucharow LLP, 2012), 1.

2. For example, the U.S. Federal Sentencing Guidelines and the American Institute of Certified Public Accountants (AICPA).

3. Frances Plimmer, "Professional Ethics—The European Code of Conduct" (presentation, 7th FIG Regional Conference, Hanoi, Vietnam, October 19-22, 2009), http://www.fig.net/pub/vietnam/papers/ts01f/ts01f_plimmer_3609.pdf; The Institute of Chartered Accountants in England and Wales, April 2012; The Institute of Certified Public Accountants in Ireland, "Code of Ethics," June 2011.

4. David Barstow, "Vast Mexico Bribery Case Hushed Up by Wal-Mart after Top-Level Struggle," *New York Times*, April 22, 2012, http://www.nytimes.com/2012/04/22/business/at-wal-mart-in-mexico-a-bribe-inquiry-silenced.html?pagewanted=all.

5. SBR Consulting, LLC, *Millennial Generation Today: Impact of the Economic Environment on Recruitment, Retention and Engagement* (SBR Consulting LLC, 2011).

Chapter 13

1. David A. Harrison and Katherine J. Klein, "What's the Difference? Diversity Constructs as Separation, Variety, or Disparity in Organizations," *Academy of Management Review* 32 (2007): 1199-1228.
2. Ibid.
3. Pelled, Lisa H., "Demographic Diversity, Conflict, and Work Group Outcomes: An Intervening Process Theory," *Organization Science* 7 (1996): 615-631; Katherine Y. Williams and Charles A. O'Reilly, III, "Demography and Diversity in Organizations: A Review of 40 Years of Research," in *Research in Organizational Behavior*, ed. Barry M. Staw and Larry L. Cummings (Greenwich, CT: JAI Press, 1998), 20: 77-140.
4. Frederick A. Miller and Judith H. Katz, *The Inclusion Breakthrough: Unleashing the Real Power of Diversity* (San Francisco: Berrett-Koehler Publishers, 2002).
5. Michael E. Mor-Barak and David A. Cherin, "A Tool to Expand Organizational Understanding of Workforce Diversity: Developing a Measure of Inclusion-Exclusion," *Administration in Social Work* 22 no. 1 (1998): 47-64.

Chapter 14

1. Jeffrey H. Dyer, Hal B. Gregersen, and Clayton M. Christensen, "The Innovator's DNA," *Harvard Business Review*, December 2009, 61-67.
2. Ibid.
3. Langdon Morris, *Innovation Metrics: The Innovation Process and How to Measure It*, An InnovationLabs White Paper (Walnut Creek, CA: InnovationLabs LLC, 2008).
4. Adam Bryant, "Want to Lead? Learn to Nurture Your Butterflies," *New York Times*, November 20, 2011, http://www.nytimes.com/ 2011/ 11/20/business/kathleen-flanagan-of-abt-on-making-confident-choices.html?pagewanted=all.
5. Adam Bryant, "Good C.E.O.'s Are Insecure (and Know It)," *New York Times*, October 10, 2010, http://www.nytimes.com/2010/10/10/ business/10corner.html?pagewanted=all.

6. SHRM Strategy and Foundation Thought Leaders Retreat, Chicago, October 2011.

7. Arun Leslie George, "Making HR the Major Driver of Organizational Innovation," presentation, the SHRM Strategy and Foundation Thought Leaders Retreat, Chicago, October 2011).

8. SHRM Foundation, "Key Takeaways from the 2011 Thought Leader Retreat," *2011 Thought Leaders Retreat: HR's Role in Managing Business Risk; Executive Summaries* (Alexandria, VA: SHRM Foundation, 2011), 3.

9. As of this writing, Apple had the largest market capitalization of any public company being traded. See Lisa Rapaport, "Apple Rises as Bernstein Sees Stock Split, Dow Membership Ahead," *Bloomberg News*, July 31, 2012.

10. Jatin DeSai, "Making HR the Major Driver of Organizational Innovation," (presentation, SHRM Foundation 2011 Thought Leaders Retreat, Chicago, October 2011.

Chapter 15

1. Julius G. Getman, Stephen B. Goldberg, and Jeanne B. Herman, "The National Labor Relations Board Voting Study: A Preliminary Report," *Journal of Legal Studies* 1, no. 2 (1972): 233-258; Julius G. Getman, Stephen B. Goldberg, and Jeanne B. Herman, *Union Representation Elections: Law and Reality* (New York: Russell Sage Foundation, 1976).

2. Herbert G. Heneman III and Marcus H. Sandver, "Predicting the Outcome of Union Certification Elections: A Review of the Literature," *Industrial and Labor Relations Review* 36, no. 4 (1983) 537-559.

3. Jack W. Wiley makes a similar point in "Six Things You Need to Know About Strategic Employee Surveys," *People & Strategy* 35, no. 1 (2012): 16-23.

4. Again, organizations need to be in compliance with the use of surveys or other interventions during negotiations or other periods specified in the union contract. Also, some countries may have limitations about how such tools can be used.

Chapter 16

1. Adi Ignatius, "The HBR Interview: 'We had to Own the Mistakes,' An interview with Howard Schultz," *Harvard Business Review*, July 2010.
2. Matias Alonzo and Peter Lacy, *A New Era of Sustainability in the Utilities Industry: UN Global Compact-Accenture CEO Study, 2010* (London, UK: Accenture, 2011).
3. TANDBERG/Ipsos MORI, *Corporate Environmental Behavior and the Impact on Brand Values* (New York, NY: TANDBERG, 2007).
4. Adam Bryant, "Good C.E.O.'s Are Insecure (and Know It)," *New York Times*, October 10, 2010, http://www.nytimes.com/2010/10/10/business/10corner.html?pagewanted=all.
5. IBS Center for Management Research, *Starbucks Human Resource Management Policies and the Growth Challenge*, Case Study Collection (Andhra Pradesh, India: IBS Center for Management Research, 2005), http://www.icmrindia.org.

Chapter 17

1. William A. Schiemann and John H. Lingle, *Bullseye!: Hitting Your Strategic Targets Through High-Impact Measurement* (New York: Free Press, 1999).
2. If you are interested in more details about the organization, the process of developing this model, the measures used, or how it was used to align their organization, see Schiemann and Lingle, *Bullseye!* (1999).
3. The model shown here is a representative view of the company's actual map but has been adapted both to protect its confidential information and to highlight points being made in this book. Some concepts shown in earlier publications are omitted here and a few added. There are some variations in naming to make them more accessible to today's reader.
4. Not the company's real name.

Chapter 18

1. Mystery shopper scores are derived from unannounced observers who come to the restaurant disguised as a customer and use a scoring system to evaluate dimensions such as cleanliness, service, or menu alignment.

Chapter 19

1. Lynne C. Lancaster and David Stillman, *When Generations Collide: Who They Are. Why They Clash. How to Solve the Generational Puzzle at Work* , (New York: HarperBusiness, 2002).
2. Thanks to Stanley M. Davis, author of *Future Perfect* (Reading, MA: Addison-Wesley, 1987), for his introduction of the term in a context related to customers.
3. Andrew Busch, "A Critical Analysis of Research Related to Workplace Retention, Satisfaction and Motivation of the Millennial Generation" (master's thesis, University of Wisconsin-Stout, 2005), http://www.uwstout.edu/lib/thesis/2005/2005buscha.pdf.
4. Although privacy regulations vary by country and are always a concern, mechanisms must be in place to protect individuals from sharing information that they would not want to be shared. As of this writing, however, employees are sharing more and more information in a variety of sites and have voluntarily made such trade-offs. Despite privacy concerns, gaining significant insights with the right data analysis while still carefully guarding employee confidential information is often possible.
5. Tamara J. Erickson and Lynda Gratton, "What It Means to Work Here," *Harvard Business Review*, March 2007.
6. Tamara Erickson, "The Real Trophy Generation," *Conference Board Review* 45 no. 5 (2008): 22.
7. Jennifer J. Deal, *Retiring the Generation Gap: How Employees Young and Old Can Find Common Ground* (San Francisco: Jossey Bass, 2006); Jennifer J. Deal, "Five Millennial Myths," *strategy+business*, February 28, 2012, http://www.strategy-business.com/article/12102?gko=0334d.

8. Adam Bryant, "Yes, Everyone Can Be Stupid for a Minute," *New York Times*, May 8, 2011, http://www.nytimes.com/2011/05/08/business/08corner.html?pagewanted=all.

9. Evernote is a provider of note-taking and archiving technology in Mountain View, California.

10. Adam Bryant, "The Phones Are Out, but the Robot Is In," *New York Times*, April 8, 2012, http://www.nytimes.com/2012/04/08/business/phil-libin-of-evernote-on-its-unusual-corporate-culture.html?pagewanted=all.

Index

About the Authors

William A. Schiemann, Ph.D. and MBA, is Chief Executive Officer of Metrus Group (www.metrus.com) in Somerville, New Jersey. Dr. Schiemann and his firm are known for their pioneering work in the creation of the People Equity (ACE) talent optimization framework, strategic performance metrics and scorecards, the strategy mapping process, valuation of internal shared service functions, and for strategic employee surveys that drive high performance.

Bill is author of *The ACE Advantage: How Smart Companies Unleash Talent for Optimal Performance* and *Reinventing Talent Management: How to Maximize Performance in the New Marketplace* and co-author of *Bullseye! Hitting Your Strategic Targets Through High-Impact Measurement*. He has also written numerous book chapters and articles for many publications, including *Conference Board Review, Applied Psychology, Journal of Business Strategy, Cost Management, Management Review, Quality Progress*, and the *Talent Management Handbook*.

Prior to the founding of Metrus Group, Inc. in 1988, Dr. Schiemann held positions in both industry and academia at such institutions as AT&T, Opinion Research Corporation, Georgia Institute of Technology, and the University of Iowa. He was former Board Chair of the SHRM Foundation, current board member with the HR Certification Institute, and is a designated Fellow and Scholar of the Society for Industrial and Organizational Psychology (SIOP).

Brian S. Morgan is Director, Organization Assessment Services at Metrus Group, Inc. He has over 30 years of experience in organization diagnostics, with particular specialization in employee survey and follow-up action planning, with a focus on strategic uses of employee surveys to predict customer satisfaction, financial performance, and other key business outcomes. His recent work also includes the design and implementation of strategic measurement system and internal customer surveys.

Dr. Morgan's work has appeared in many publications, including the *Harvard Business Review, Handbook of Business Strategy, Quality Progress, Change Management Handbook, Strategy and Leadership, The Journal of Applied Psychology,* and *The Journal of Strategic Performance Measurement,* among others. He co-authored the chapter on Strategic Employee Surveys in *Getting Results from Employee Surveys,* edited by Alan Kraut.

He holds a B.A. in Psychology and an M.S. in Industrial Psychology from San Francisco State University and a Ph.D. in Social Psychology from Wayne State University.

Jerry H. Seibert, MA is Principal and Vice President of Diagnostic Services of Metrus Group. He has 25 years of experience working with organizations to measure and improve customer, employee, and other stakeholder perceptions. He has also led numerous large field studies on internal customer service/value, and its connection to business outcomes.

Jerry is the author of many articles on employee and customer perception measurement, including a series with the American Society for Quality on internal service/value, published in *Quality Progress.*

Prior to Metrus Group he was the President of the research and consulting firm Parkside Associates and CEO of software developer rL Solutions.

Additional SHRM-Published Books

The ACE Advantage: How Smart Companies Unleash Talent for Optimal Performance
William A. Schiemann

Becoming the Evidence-Based Manager: Making the Science of Management Work for You
Gary P. Latham

Business Literacy Survival Guide for HR Professionals
Regan W. Garey

Business-Focused HR: 11 Processes to Drive Results
Scott P. Mondore, Shane S. Douthitt, and Marissa A. Carson

The Chief HR Officer: Defining the New Role of Human Resource Leaders
Patrick M. Wright, John W. Boudreau, David A. Pace, Elizabeth "Libby" Sartain, Paul McKinnon, Richard L. Antoine (eds.)

The Cultural Fit Factor: Creating an Employment Brand That Attracts, Retains, and Repels the Right Employees
Lizz Pellet

From Hello to Goodbye: Proactive Tips for Maintaining Positive Employee Relations
Christine V. Walters

HR at Your Service: Lessons from Benchmark Service Organizations
Gary P. Latham and Robert C. Ford

Human Resource Essentials: Your Guide to Starting and Running the HR Function
Lin Grensing-Pophal

Leading with Your Heart: Diversity and *Ganas* for Inspired Inclusion
Cari M. Dominguez and Judith Sotherlund

The Manager's Guide to HR: Hiring, Firing, Performance Evaluations, Documentation, Benefits, and Everything Else You Need to Know
Max Muller

Point Counterpoint: New Perspectives on People & Strategy
Anna Tavis, Richard Vosburgh, Ed Gubman (eds.)

The Power of Stay Interviews for Engagement and Retention
Richard P. Finnegan

Proving the Value of HR: How and Why to Measure ROI
Jack J. Phillips and Patricia Pulliam Phillips

Reinventing Diversity: Transforming Organizational Community to Strengthen People, Purpose and Performance
Howard J. Ross

Reinventing Talent Management: How to Maximize Performance in the New Marketplace
William A. Schiemann

Rethinking Retention in Good Times and Bad: Breakthrough Ideas for Keeping Your Best Workers
Richard P. Finnegan

Stop Bullying at Work: Strategies and Tools for HR and Legal Professionals
Teresa A. Daniel

Transformational Diversity: Why and How Intercultural Competencies Can Help Organizations to Survive and Thrive
Fiona Citkin and Lynda Spielman

Workflex: The Essential Guide to Effective and Flexible Workplaces
Families and Work Institute and Society for Human Resource Management